Poems

Antonia Pozzi

Translated by Peter Robinson

ALMA CLASSICS

THE PUBLISHER WOULD LIKE TO DEDICATE THIS BOOK TO
JOHN CALDER
FOR FIRST PUBLISHING ANTONIA POZZI IN ENGLISH

ALMA CLASSICS LTD
Hogarth House
32-34 Paradise Road
Richmond
Surrey TW9 1SE
United Kingdom
www.almaclassics.com

This book is published with the support of the Italian Ministry of
Foreign Affairs

First published by Alma Classics Limited (previously Oneworld Classics
Limited) in 2011
This new edition first published by Alma Classics Limited in 2015
Introduction, translation and notes © Peter Robinson 2011
Italian texts © Estate of Antonia Pozzi 2011
Cover image: Anna Omelchenko / 123RF

Printed in Great Britain by CPI Group (UK) Ltd, Croydon CR0 4YY

ISBN: 978–1–84749–470–2

Antonia Pollin

Contents

CONTENTS

Introduction

THE MARCH 1955 EDITION of the *London Magazine* included three lyrics by Antonia Pozzi, in translations by Nora Wydenbruck. The publication also contained the following contributor's note on a page headed 'In Case You Didn't Know':

> ANTONIA POZZI was born in Milan on 13th February 1912, and died there on 3rd December 1938. She studied languages and literature at Milan University and received the degree of D.Litt., as well as the Gold Medal of the Fondazione Donati for her thesis on Flaubert. The poems she began to write at the age of seventeen were not seen by anyone in her lifetime, but were found, after her death, by her parents and published in 1939. Today these poems are to be found in most anthologies of modern Italian poetry and even in the schoolbooks.[1]

While not exactly untrue, at least two of these statements are not as true as they might have been. She didn't simply "die", but, on 2nd December, travelled out towards Chiaravalle in countryside to the south-east of Milan, and took poison. She was discovered in a state of collapse, but from which she could not be revived, dying the following day. Nor is it true that her poems "were not seen by anyone in her lifetime". In a letter to Vittorio Sereni dated 20th June 1935, she refers to "the Antonia of the poems",[2] suggesting that he at least was familiar with her work before her death. Nor were the notebooks her parents found quite the works that were "published in 1939".

Antonia Pozzi was born in Milan, the only child of a dominating lawyer father, the mayor of Pasturo, a mountain village in the Valsassina, some fifty miles north-east of the Lombard capital. She began composing personal verse in standard metres when she was seventeen, echoing the work of poets such as Giovanni Pascoli and Guido Gozzano. While still at school she was introduced to more recent poetry, by poets little known now, such as Annunzio Cervi and Tullio Gadenz, sustaining a correspondence with the latter.[3] She confided her poetry to school friends, including Elvira Gandini and Lucia Bozzi, the second of whom copied and preserved after Pozzi's death accurate texts for much of her work.

Though Pozzi began to explore the possibilities of poetic expression in a received style, from the first there is an individual urgency of utterance, of self-confession. The thought of personal extinction runs through these poems like a vein, from an almost morbidly envious devotion to the dead of the Great War – something that figures in 'Offerta a una tomba' ('Offering to a Tomb'), 'Sventatezza' ('Heedlessness'), and 'In un cimitero di guerra' ('In a War Cemetery') here – to a personal depression and sense of emptiness in European culture as it slides precipitously towards the outbreak of a second global conflict. Indeed, Pozzi's poetry can be read as an almost uninterrupted dialogue with the thought of death. Even her love affair with Antonio Maria Cervi, her Classics teacher, recounted here in the sequence entitled 'La vita sognata' ('The Dreamed Life'), was figured around their desire to have a child who would be baptized to perpetuate the memory of Cervi's brother Annunzio, who had died in uniform.

Pozzi was quick to see the importance of the free verse pioneered by Giuseppe Ungaretti in his early volume of war poetry, *Allegria di naufragi* (1919), from which she may well have adopted the habit of dating and often locating her poems, and in his second book *Sentimento del tempo* (1933). Critics have also seen traces of Salvatore Quasimodo and Eugenio

Montale, while Umberto Saba's *Cose leggere e vaganti* seems to be echoed in her title 'Desiderio di cose leggere' ('Desire for Light Things'). She was a fine and ambitious student, reading the poetry of T.S. Eliot, Paul Valéry and Rainer Maria Rilke in both translation and the original. While at university in Milan she came into contact with a circle of young writers and poets who were students of the philosopher Antonio Banfi. Among the important friends and colleagues with whom she corresponded were Clelia and Ottavia Abate, Alba Binda, Remo Cantoni, Dino Formaggio, Alberto Mondadori, Enzo Paci and Vittorio Sereni.

Pozzi's poetry developed rapidly after 1935, something that can be attributed in no small part to her literary relationship with the last of these, Vittorio Sereni. The economy of expression and obliquity of method introduced by the poets associated with Hermeticism also contributed to the precision and concreteness of her later work, her poems being ever more firmly occasioned in perception and her immediate surroundings. Though the 1930s were not a time when poetry of protest was encouraged, nevertheless there are indications of her lack of sympathy for the regime in verse written after 1935, such as 'Le donne' ('The Women'), a period when Italy's neo-imperial foreign policy and war in Eritrea pointed ever more inevitably towards its involvement in the coming European war. Towards the end of her life she worked as a high-school teacher at the Liceo Schiaparelli in Milan, and also undertook voluntary social work in a poor quarter of the city. While both of these activities indicate a desire to become involved constructively in the lives of others, and of those less fortunate, neither experience appears to have been sufficient to alleviate her inner turmoil.

From this distance, her economically comfortable life in the 1930s might seem a charmed one, including travels all over Italy, with visits to France, England, Germany, Austria, Greece and North Africa. Yet there were heavy expectations upon her, both those that arose from her personal and social sensitivity and her various artistic talents, and those put upon her by family and friends to succeed and fulfil the roles then expected of a young bourgeois lady. Her devotion to mountaineering excursions – she was a member of the Club Alpino Italiano – may have derived some of its passion from the temporary escape it occasioned from the culturally contradictory demands she felt. Such expectations appear to have resulted in a fierce splitting, expressed in a letter to Sereni of 20th June 1935:

> But one day you said something that gnaws at me terribly today: you told me I'm very noble, that I *don't know* what vulgarity is. If you saw me today, Vittorio: what a tremendous crack has opened within me, what a tumble. On one side the Antonia of the poems and the good principles, on the other a person without will and without centre, who listens to the most brutal talk without reacting, and when the eyes before her grow cynical – neither fraternal nor compassionate any longer – she doesn't get up, doesn't go away, but remains like one hypnotized awaiting those caresses she knows are given her – not out of pity – but as a game, a stupid game that costs nothing and can cost a life.[4]

"I feel myself more than ever Tonia Kröger", she writes in the same letter, identifying with the eponymous male character in Thomas Mann's 1903 story. Tonio "bore within himself the possibilities of a thousand different ways of life, together with the secret awareness that they were all impossibilities", or, elsewhere, he "wrote poems and couldn't even answer what in the world he wanted to be", believing that "an artist must virtually die in order to be fully creative".[5] Added to such ideas were her then inappropriate political sympathies. Among her friends were Paolo and Pietro Treves, brothers who had to leave Italy in 1938 because of the Racial Laws, the former directing the "Radio Londra" broadcasts from England during World War Two.

"I stand between two worlds" and "am at home in neither",[6] writes Tonio to his friend Lisaveta at the end of Mann's story. Pozzi's suicide appears, then, to have resulted from her inability to integrate, or at least accommodate, her creative aspirations and emotional needs with the family's expectations for her. At the same time, her senses of moral, social and political good were in more than tacit conflict with the apparent victory of Fascist power in the wake of the Pact of Steel, allying Italy and Nazi Germany, and of the Munich Crisis. The latter's resolution in September 1938, which avoided war while achieving Hitler's aims, was represented in her country as a diplomatic triumph for Mussolini. It is likely, then, that the international tension increasing during late 1938 combined with her personal conflicts to aggravate beyond bearing the desperation and depression that finally led the poet to take her own life.

A manuscript copy of Sereni's early poem 'Diana', which ends with "the song" that "breathes on the memory / to reprove you for dying",[7] was found on her body. At the foot of the poem she had scrawled "*Addio Vittorio, caro* – my dear brother. You'll remember me together with Maria".[8] Yet even the wording of this last note has been contested, Graziella Bernabò preferring the interpretation of her hand by Onorina Dino, who believes it reads not "with Maria", for Maria Luisa Bonfanti, but "with Manzi" referring to the friend of both poets, Gianluigi Manzi, who had himself committed suicide in 1935.[9] Sereni, though, who was shown the note, believed that it was addressed both to him and his future wife, writing to her on 16th November 1939: "Poor Antonia. Her blessing is upon us two, and for me that last cry of hers no longer contains anything tragic. It remains suspended like a tender word, convincing for all of the life that remains to me."[10] Sereni had, in fact, written an editorial note for an issue of the literary magazine *Corrente* dated 31st December 1938, a publication closed down by the authorities when war was declared in June 1940:

We lost her on 3rd December last, in the evening. And though we remember her here for the benefit of those who a while ago read her article appearing in these columns, quite different words would be fitting between us who knew her. She was twenty-six years old and had graduated three years back with a work – preferring not to say: a thesis – on Flaubert that we hope to be able to read in print some day or other. Most of all for us, so that it may deceive us as to the brevity of her time on this earth.[11]

Though the note struck here is of her loss to a literary group and its magazine circle, by the time Sereni came to compose an elegiac poem for her, two years later, her death had become associated with the cultural and political entrapment of his entire generation, one that had by then taken them across the shadow line into war. Sereni's elegy has no indication of its subject, beside the second-person address, its being named after her death day, '3 dicembre', and the discreet allusions to Pozzi's poems that scholars have since underlined in their notes:

> At the final tumult of these lines
> peace comes to you, where the city,
> in a flight of bridges and avenues
> hurls itself into the country
> and those who pass don't know
> of you just as you don't know
> about the echoes of the hunts grazing you.

> Peace perhaps is truly yours
> and the eyes we closed
> forever now reopened
> are astonished
> that still for us
> you die a little every year
> on this particular day.[12]

Sereni's touches on a number of Pozzi's poems, including 'La porta che si chiude' ('The Closing Door') of 1931, which ends with her wish to find peace, and 'Fine di una domenica' ('A Sunday's End') from 1937. The "echoes of the hunts" in Sereni's poem may allude to the fact that her father, Roberto Pozzi, was a keen hunter, but they also foreshadow conflicts both personal and public grazing her when alive, ones that she can now no longer hear or feel.

After the poet's death, Roberto Pozzi used his connections with figures in the Milanese literary scene such as Sereni to set about gaining for his daughter Antonia the literary reputation that she had barely started to achieve, resulting in the publication of *Parole* in 1939. The success of his efforts is demonstrated by Montale's preface to a new edition of *Parole* published in 1948, which confirmed that the book deserved to be included in Mondadori's "Lo Specchio" series of significant contemporary poetry and "to await the judgement of the future".[13]

However, her father's selecting and editing of some poems – doubtless an act of memorial piety – has been seen by her later editors Alessandra Cenni and Onorina Dino as patriarchal meddling. In particular, they note the suppression of references to Antonia's passion for Antonio Maria Cervi, to whom she gave copies of poems with dedications that in Cenni and Dino's later Garzanti editions (and here) have been restored. Pozzi's father even destroyed her last "Testament", dated 1st December 1938, which, reconstructed from his memory, has now been published.[14] It is not impossible that the note was destroyed to allow their daughter a Christian burial, and then partially reconstructed after that ritual had been safely achieved. Despite the natural desire to place blame for her suicide upon the over-zealous devotion of her parents, the grief of those same parents should surely not be underestimated, nor should their efforts, more successful than her father might have imagined, to find for their daughter the readership that both they and Sereni saw her poetry as deserving.

In the unlikely event of Sereni not having been shown at least some of Pozzi's poems before her death, by 1940 her father had contacted him about making the work as widely known as possible. Sereni's letters to the family, written between May 1939 and July 1964, concerning the printing and noticing of her poems have been published.[15] These efforts to have her work widely known extended, as we have seen, to the publication of translations in a number of European countries, and Nora Wydenbruck acknowledges the hospitality of the Pozzi family at Pasturo during her work on the English translations for John Calder's 1955 edition.

Wydenbruck's translations are, however, compromised by the fact that the Italian texts she used had been interfered with by Roberto Pozzi, and also because the selection – which may not have been made by the translator herself – tends to underline the "Antonia of the poems and good principles" referred to in the letter to Sereni, thereby presenting a rather sanitized image of the poet. This is most notable in relation to the set of poems called 'La vita sognata' ('The Dreamed Life'), which deal with Pozzi's relationship with Antonio Maria Cervi, a relationship that her father had disapproved of, forbidding them to meet and probably arranging for Cervi to be transferred to Rome. The first poem in the sequence, also called 'La vita sognata', has six lines in its second stanza in Wydenbruck's translation, while the authoritative Garzanti editions have nine. The missing three are: "*tu cui un'onda bianca / di tristezza cadeva sul volto / se ti chiamavo con labbra impure*" ("you to whom a white wave / of sadness fell across the face / if I called you with impure lips"). Perhaps it was the "*labbra impure*" that prompted this edit. In the definitive editions four further poems are added to the six in Wydenbruck's selection, all addressed to Cervi. Furthermore, the touches of daily reality and social circumstance that some of Pozzi's works include – such as the emblematic "*stridono*

/ *due sigarette spente in una pozza*" ("two cigarettes / shriek extinguished in a puddle") of 'Periferia' ('Outskirts') – do not appear in Wydenbruck's translations, either because they were not chosen, or in more than one case because they were suppressed by means of local cuts.

The Calder edition also included 'A Portrait of Antonia' by the novelist Raffaele Calzini (1885–1953), too saccharine to be readable now: "I used to call Antonia 'the youthful Sappho': there was a strange aura of spirituality around her smiling and yet melancholy face, and beneath her deceptively fair and childlike appearance I could sense a passionate and ardent spirit."[16] The original presentation of the poet to English readers aggravated thus the splitting she suffered by effacing her "vulgar" side, as much an inspiration for her almost unbroken poetic output as her apparent lack of vulgarity in finer feeling and poetry.

However, though Roberto Pozzi's editing leaves the Calder volume flawed, many of the poems translated are not substantially different from those in the most recent editions. 'Morte di una stagione' ('Death of a Season'), for instance, differs from them only in failing to include place and date of composition ("*Pasturo, 20 settembre 1937*") at the foot of the text. And it should be remembered that, though not always textually reliable, Wydenbruck's edition introduced for the first time to English readers this significant poet's work, becoming a historical document in the process by which Antonia Pozzi was transformed from an unknown figure into one now recognized for her contribution to modern Italian poetry in the earlier part of her century.

For those who would like to compare the translations published here with others, *Breath: Poems and Letters* (2002), translated by Lawrence Venuti, fluently renders Pozzi's poetry as if it were the work of American poets such as H.D., Amy Lowell, Mina Loy or perhaps Lorine Niedecker. Venuti articulately regrets the fact that she did not belong to a movement of uninhibited experimental writers: "in establishing this connection", he affirms, "the English supplies what she lacked in Italian: a tradition of modernist women poets."[17] While it is perfectly true that she did not belong to such a group, the application to her life situation and literary possibilities of expectations from another tradition in effect downplays the movement that she did belong to, namely the one formed around the philosopher Antonio Banfi at the University of Milan, which enabled her to form close links with a number of poets of her own age, the most important of whom was to be Sereni. She similarly had models whose influence appears in her work, such as, most significantly, the Ungaretti already mentioned, who foreshadows her lineation and is echoed in a number of poems, or, perhaps, Emily Dickinson, from whom she may have evolved her use of dashes. Venuti, therefore, although no less well meaning than the poet's father, in adapting her poems makes them appear in translation works they never were, nor could have been. A final reflection on Venuti's experiment is that it runs the risk of denying to anglophone readers the possibility of intuiting in translation the precise lineaments of a sensibility manifested in the art of another literary culture. To my mind, this is the imaginative gift that poetry translation should strive at all costs to offer and to this end I have allowed my versions to sound as near to the Italian in English as possible.

Nora Wydenbruck wrote in her brief preface that the "best verse translation can never be more than a 'crib', and even the reader who does not possess Italian should look at the original text in order to get the full enjoyment of Antonia's word-music, although English is perhaps the language best adapted to imitate the terseness and render the delicate overtones of her diction."[18] Wydenbruck's translations are fairly criticized by Venuti, who judges that her English "inflates and exoticizes".[19] It might equally be said that she renders Pozzi's poetry into a conventionally euphemistic idiom characteristic of some poetry written rather more than half a century ago. Venuti's versions effectively pitch Pozzi's poetry at the tonal level of American modernist writing, and so naturalize her work to the expectations of a poetry-reading public for whom, say, William Carlos Williams's accent is an accepted norm. Venuti's selection acknowledges the importance of the affair with Antonio Maria Cervi for her poetic development, though he only translates a few of the sequence 'La vita sognata', which directly addresses their separation, interspersing them among poems on other subjects.

What the evolution of her poetry shows, I believe, is a growing confidence in the expressive adequacy of circumstantial detail, embodying her nervously muted awareness of conflicted domestic and international realities, increasing as the decade of the 1930s draws to its close. The women's movement in Italy has, as is right and proper, contributed to the revaluation of Pozzi's work, and to her being freed from the sanitized image that had significantly mischaracterized her work. Though there were, *pace* Venuti, significant twentieth-century women writers who come before her, Ada Negri and Sibilla Aleramo for example, and contemporaries too, such as Daria Mendicanti, who belonged to Banfi's circle, Antonia Pozzi is now understood to be the most significant poet to confront the contradictions of being a gifted young woman in the 1930s, and by her example she paved the way for a flourishing of Italian women's poetry in the second half of the century. Still, it is equally worth recalling that the sense of loss expressed in Sereni's obituary written for *Corrente* is one felt by a group of young writers, critics and artists not exclusively of either gender. The development in Pozzi's poetry of an individual rhythmic pulse and a conjoining of the perceiving self with an acutely circumscribed space, inspired by the work of Ungaretti and Quasimodo, as well as the fraternal influence of early Sereni poems, surely locate her work among the pioneer poets of what would be described, after the war, as the "*linea lombarda*", the Lombard Line in

Italian twentieth-century verse. And this is where her poetry properly belongs.

A further edition of *Parole*, prepared for publication by Vittorio Sereni, appeared from Mondadori in 1964, but this was to be the last collection of her work to appear in print for over twenty years. A revival of interest in Pozzi's poetry began in 1986 with the appearance of Alessandra Cenni and Onorina Dino's edition of *La vita sognata e altre poesie inedite*. The efforts of Cenni and Dino to establish an authoritative text of her poetry then produced a new edition of *Parole* (1989). This work has since gone through a number of revised editions, the most recent of which, *Tutte le opere*, edited by Cenni, appeared in 2009, and has been used in making the translations for this edition.

My translations aim to be rhythmically alive and written in a fresh English, yet at the same time to form accurate renderings of the poems, including faithful representations of her metrical patterns, punctuation and disposition on the page. My attempts have had to confront one particular difficulty: being the poems of a privileged young woman coming to poetic maturity during the 1930s, they often have a passionately refined vulnerability in contemporary English that might be compared to the high-pitched expressiveness of an operatic soprano. As I have observed, there already exist translations that aim to present a Pozzi whose poems in English display as little of this characteristic as they can. Here, in attempting to present her poetry as accurately as possible, I have also embraced this aspect of her work, and attempted translations that make it audible but with as little off-putting shrillness as is compatible with accuracy. This has been attempted not by means of an overall stylistic strategy, but by renderings of local features which try to stay close to the Italian in as vivid an English as I am able to manage.

I have taken note of the rebalancing of her work expressed by Venuti's selection, and have included my own versions of some poems also rendered in his edition. 'La vita sognata' appears here in a complete translation and as a distinct sequence, placed after the poems of *Parole*, as in Cenni's most recent Italian edition. The selection published here represents Pozzi's poetry at every stage of her development, and includes some of the until recently uncollected poems and drafts from *Tutte le opere* (2009).

Antonia Pozzi clearly treated poetry as a constant companion, writing poems in some years on a near daily basis, years such as 1929, 1933 and 1934. And it might be worth noting the extent to which poetry appears to have come less often during the last year or so of her brief life. To compare the oeuvre of her short existence with the single book of poems, *Frontiera* (1941), that Sereni produced over those years is to get a sense of the prolific and almost unbroken outpouring of poetry to which she dedicated herself. I hope that readers will feel that this selection of her work adequately represents her poetry at its best.

– Peter Robinson

Notes to the Introduction

1. *The March 1955 edition... in the schoolbooks*: *The London Magazine*, vol. 2, No. 3 (March 1955), p. 110. Wydenbruck's translations of the three poems, 'Snowfields', 'The Wide Plain' and 'Africa', appeared later the same year in *Poems*, published by John Calder.

2. *letter to Vittorio Sereni... Antonia of the poems*: Antonia Pozzi, *Tutte le opere*, ed. Alessandra Cenni (Milan: Garzanti, 2009), p. 522.

3. *Tullio Gadenz... correspondence with the latter*: See Antonia Pozzi, *L'età delle parole è finita: Lettere 1927–1938*, ed. Alessandra Cenni and Onorina Dino (Milan: Rosellina Archinto, 1989), and Lawrence Venuti, 'Versions of Antonia Pozzi', in Antonia Pozzi, *Breath: Poems and Letters*, trans. Lawrence Venuti (Middletown, CT: Wesleyan University Press, 2002), pp. 175–77. Venuti includes a poem by Gadenz on p. 193.

4. *But one day... cost a life*: Pozzi, *Tutte le opere*, p. 522.

5. *bore within himself... in order to be fully creative*: Thomas Mann, 'Tonio Kröger', *Death in Venice and Other Tales*, trans. Joachim Neugroschel (Harmondsworth: Penguin Books, 1999), pp. 180, 181, 183.

6. *I stand between two worlds... at home in neither*: Ibid. p. 227.

7. *the song... reprove you for dying*: Vittorio Sereni, *The Selected Poetry and Prose*, trans. Peter Robinson and Marcus Perryman (Chicago: University of Chicago Press, 2006), p. 55.

8. *Addio Vittorio... together with Maria*: Antonia Pozzi and Vittorio Sereni, *La giovinezza che non trova scampo: Poesie e lettere degli anni trenta*, ed. Alessandra Cenni (Milan: Scheiwiller, 1995), p. 45.

9. *Yet even the wording... committed suicide in 1935*: See Graziella Bernabò, *Per troppa vita che ho nel sangue:*

Antonia Pozzi e la sua poesia (Milan: Viennepierre edizioni, 2004), p. 294 and note 42 on pp. 299–300.

10. *Poor Antonia… that remains to me*: Vittorio Sereni, *Poesie*, ed. Dante Isella (Milan: Mondadori, 1995), p. 330.

11. *We lost her on 3rd December… brevity of her time on this earth*: *Luino e immediati dintorni: geografie poetiche di Vittorio Sereni*, ed. Angelo Stella and Barbara Colli (Varese: Insubria University Press, 2010), p. 57.

12. *At the final tumult… on this particular day*: Sereni, *Selected Poetry and Prose*, p. 57.

13. *Montale's preface… judgement of the future*: Eugenio Montale, *Sulla poesia*, ed. Giorgio Zampa (Milan: Mondadori, 1976), p. 52.

14. *her last "Testament"… now been published*: See Pozzi, *L'età delle parole è finita*, pp. 271–72.

15. *Sereni's letters… have been published*: See Pozzi and Sereni, *La giovinezza che non trova scampo*, pp. 77–107. Sereni's contribution to the publishing of Pozzi's work is also noted in Gian Carlo Ferretti, *Poeta e di poeti funzionario: Il lavoro editoriale di Vittorio Sereni* (Milan: il Saggiatore, 1999), p. 125.

16. *I used to call Antonia… passionate and ardent spirit*: Raffaele Calzini, 'A Portrait of Antonia', in Antonia Pozzi, *Poems*, trans. Nora Wydenbruck (London: John Calder, 1955), p. 221.

17. *in establishing this connection… modernist women poets*: Lawrence Venuti, 'Versions of Antonia Pozzi', *Breath: Poems and Letters*, p. xxii.

18. *best verse translation… overtones of her diction*: Nora Wydenbruck, 'Preface', Pozzi, *Poems* (1955), n.p. [ii].

19. *inflates and exoticizes*: Venuti, 'Versions of Antonia Pozzi', *Breath: Poems and Letters*, p. xxi.

Poems

*Se le mie parole potessero
essere offerte a qualcuno
questa pagina
porterebbe il tuo nome.*

*If my words could
be offered to someone
this page
would bear your name.*

PAROLE / WORDS

Offerta a una tomba

ad A.M.C.

Dall'alto mi hai mostrato,   I
un po' fuori della frana ruinosa di case,
un additare nero di cipressi
saettati attraverso l'azzurro
a custodire
i marmi bianchi del cimitero.
Ho pensato ad una tomba
che non ho mai veduta
e mi è sembrato
di deporvi in quell'istante,   10
con trepido cuore a fior di mani,
un vivo fascio
di garofani rossi.

17 aprile 1929

Offering to a Tomb

to A.M.C.*

From high above you showed me,   1
not far beyond the houses' ruinous slide,
a black pointing of cypresses
darting through the azure
as custodian
to the cemetery's white marble.
I thought of a tomb
I've never seen
and to me it seemed
there I placed at that moment,   10
with tremulous heart on my sleeve,
a living clutch
of red carnations.

17th April 1929

Un'altra sosta

a L.B.

Appoggiami la testa sulla spalla: I
ch'io ti carezzi con un gesto lento,
come se la mia mano accompagnasse
una lunga, invisibile gugliata.
Non sul tuo capo solo: su ogni fronte
che dolga di tormento e di stanchezza
scendono queste mie carezze cieche,
come foglie ingiallite d'autunno
in una pozza che riflette il cielo.

Milano, 23 aprile 1929

Another Respite

to L.B.*

Rest your head on my shoulder: I
so I caress you with a slow gesture,
as if my hand accompanied
a long, invisible needleful of thread.
Not on your face only: on any forehead
aching with torment and tiredness
fall these blind caresses of mine,
like the yellowed leaves of autumn
in a puddle reflecting the sky.

Milan, 23rd April 1929

Amore di lontananza

Ricordo che, quand'ero nella casa   1
della mia mamma, in mezzo alla pianura,
avevo una finestra che guardava
sui prati; in fondo, l'argine boscoso
nascondeva il Ticino e, ancor più in fondo,
c'era una striscia scura di colline.
Io allora non avevo visto il mare
che una sol volta, ma ne conservavo
un'aspra nostalgia da innamorata.
Verso sera fissavo l'orizzonte;   10
socchiudevo un po' gli occhi; accarezzavo
i contorni e i colori tra le ciglia:
e la striscia dei colli si spianava,
tremula, azzurra: a me pareva il mare
e mi piaceva più del mare vero.

Milano, 24 aprile 1929

Love of Distance*

I remember, when in my mother's house,   1
in the middle of the plain, I had
a window that looked onto
the meadows; far off, the wooded bank
hid the Ticino and, further on,
there was a dark line of hills.
Back then I'd only seen the sea
one time, but preserved of it
a sharp nostalgia as when in love.
Towards evening I stared at the skyline;   10
narrowed my eyes a little; caressed
outlines and colours between my lids;
and the line of hills flattened out,
trembling, azure: and seemed the sea to me
and pleased me more than the real sea.

Milan, 24th April 1929

Distacco

a T.F.

Tu, partita. 1
Senza desiderare la parola
che avevo in cuore e che non seppi dire.
Nel vano della porta, il nostro bacio
(lieve, ché ti eri appena incipriata)
quasi spaccato in due da un gran barbaglio
di luce, che veniva dalle scale.
Io rimasta
lungamente al mio tavolo, dinnanzi
a un vecchio ritrattino della mamma, 10
specchiando fissamente dentro il vetro
i miei occhi febbrili, inariditi.

Milano, 9 maggio 1929

Separation

to T. F.*

You, departed.   1
Without wishing the word
I had in my heart and could not say.
In the space of the door, our kiss
(light, for you'd just powdered your face)
near split in two by a great glare
of light, which came from the stairs.
Me, remained
a long time at my table, before
an old miniature of my mother,   10
fixedly regarding in the glass
my feverish, dried eyes.

Milan, 9th May 1929

Sventatezza

Ricordo un pomeriggio di settembre,   1
sul Montello. Io, ancora una bambina,
col trecciolino smilzo ed un prurito
di pazze corse su per le ginocchia.
Mio padre, rannicchiato dentro un andito
scavato in un rialzo del terreno,
mi additava attraverso una fessura
il Piave e le colline; mi parlava
della guerra, di sé, dei suoi soldati.
Nell'ombra, l'erba gelida e affilata   10
mi sfiorava i polpacci: sotto terra,
le radici succhiavan forse ancora
qualche goccia di sangue. Ma io ardevo
dal desiderio di scattare fuori,
nell'invadente sole, per raccogliere
un pugnetto di more da una siepe.

Milano, 22 maggio 1929

Heedlessness

I remember a September afternoon   1
on the Montello.* Me, a child still,
with a little thin plait and an itch
for crazy races up through my knees.
My father, crouched within a passage
dug into some rising terrain,
indicated for me through a cleft,
the Piave and hills; he spoke to me
of the war, of himself, his soldiers.
In the shadow, the sharp and frozen grass   10
was grazing my calves: underground,
the roots were perhaps still sucking
up some drops of blood. But me I burned
with the desire to leap outside,
into the invading sun, to gather
a fistful of blackberries from a hedge.

Milano, 22nd May 1929

13

Giacere

Ora l'annientamento blando   1
di nuotare riversa,
col sole in viso
– il cervello penetrato di rosso
traverso le palpebre chiuse –.
Stasera, sopra il letto, nella stessa postura,
il candore trasognato
di bere,
con le pupille larghe,
l'anima bianca della notte.   10

Santa Margherita, 19 giugno 1929

Lying Down

Now the bland annihilation   1
of swimming backstroke,
with sun on my face
– the brain pierced by red
through eyelids closed –.
Tonight, on my bed, in the same posture,
the dreamy candour
of drinking,
with dilated pupils,
the white soul of the night.   10

Santa Margherita,* 19th June 1929

Filosofia

Non trovo più il mio libro di filosofia.   1
Tiravo in carrettino
un marmocchio di otto mesi – robetta molle, saliva, sorrisino –.
Quel che m'ingombrava le mani, l'ho buttato via.

Il fratellino di quel bimbetto,
a due anni, è caduto in una caldaia d'acqua bollente:
in ventiquattro ore è morto, atrocemente.
Il parroco è sicuro che è diventato un angioletto.

La sua mamma non ha voluto andare al cimitero
a vedere dove gliel'hanno sotterrato.   10
Pei contadini, il lutto è un lusso smodato:
la sua mamma non veste di nero.

Ma, quando quest'ultima creaturina,
con le manine, le pizzica il viso,
ella cerca il suo antico sorriso:
e trova soltanto un riso velato – un povero riso in sordina.

Oggi, da una donna, ho sentito
che quella mamma, in chiesa, non ci vuole più andare.
Stasera non posso studiare,
perché il libro di filosofia l'ho smarrito.   20

Carnisio, 7 luglio 1929

Philosophy

My philosophy book I can no longer find.   1
I was pulling in the cart
an eight-month-old mite – soft stuff, saliva, little smile –.
What encumbered my hand, I threw away.

At two, that baby's younger brother fell
into a boiler of scalding water:
he was dead, horridly, within a day.
The parish priest's sure he's become a little angel.

His mother wouldn't go to the cemetery
to see where they buried him for her.   10
Black his mother doesn't wear:
for country folk mourning is an outmoded luxury.

But when this other little creature
pinches her face with tiny hands,
in search of her old smile, she finds
only a veiled one – a poor muted feature.

Today, from a woman I heard
that mother wouldn't go into church any more.
This evening I can't study, for
my philosophy book I have mislaid.   20

Carnisio,* 7th July 1929

Vicenda d'acque

La mia vita era come una cascata   1
inarcata nel vuoto;
la mia vita era tutta incoronata
di schiumate e di spruzzi.
Gridava la follia d'inabissarsi
in profondità cieca;
rombava la tortura di donarsi,
in veemente canto,
in offerta ruggente,
al vorace mistero del silenzio.   10

Ed ora la mia vita è come un lago
scavato nella roccia;
l'urlo della caduta è solo un vago
mormorio, dal profondo.
Oh, lascia ch'io m'allarghi in blandi cerchi
di glauca dolcezza:
lascia ch'io mi riposi dei soverchi
balzi e ch'io taccia, infine:
poi che una culla e un'eco
ho trovate nel vuoto e nel silenzio   20

Milano, 28 novembre 1929

Event of Waters

My life was like a cascade   1
arched into the void;
my life was entirely crowned
with froth and with spray.
There cried the folly of plunging
into blind depths;
there rumbled the torture of giving
yourself in vehement song,
in roaring gift,
to the voracious enigma of silence.   10

And now my life is like a lake
hollowed in the rock;
the cry of the fall is just a vague
murmur, from the deep.
Oh, let me spread out in bland rings
of glaucous softness:
let me rest from too much
leaping and be mute, at last:
since a cradle and an echo
I've found in the void and silence.   20

Milan, 28th November 1929

Novembre

E poi – se accadrà ch'io me ne vada –   1
resterà qualchecosa
di me
nel mio mondo –
resterà un'esile scìa di silenzio
in mezzo alle voci –
un tenue fiato di bianco
in cuore all'azzurro –

Ed una sera di novembre
una bambina gracile   10
all'angolo d'una strada
venderà tanti crisantemi
e ci saranno le stelle
gelide verdi remote –
Qualcuno piangerà
chissà dove – chissà dove –
Qualcuno cercherà i crisantemi
per me
nel mondo
quando accadrà che senza ritorno   20
io me ne debba andare.

Milano, 29 ottobre 1930

November

And then – if it happens I go away –   1
there'll remain something
of me
in my world –
there'll remain a slender wake of silence
amid the voices –
a tenuous breath of white
at the heart of azure –

And one November evening
a frail little girl   10
at a street corner
will sell so many chrysanthemums
and there'll be the stars
ice-cold, green, remote –
Someone will cry
who knows where – who knows where –
Someone will search out chrysanthemums
for me
in the world
when it happens that without return   20
I'll have to go away.

Milan, 29th October 1930

Presagio

Esita l'ultima luce   I
fra le dita congiunte dei pioppi –
l'ombra trema di freddo e d'attesa
dietro di noi
e lenta muove intorno le braccia
per farci più soli –

Cade l'ultima luce
sulle chiome dei tigli –
in cielo le dita dei pioppi
s'inanellano di stelle –   10

Qualcosa dal cielo discende
verso l'ombra che trema –
qualcosa passa
nella tenebra nostra
come un biancore –
forse qualcosa che ancora
non è –
forse qualcuno che sarà
domani –
forse una creatura   20
del nostro pianto –

Milano, 15 novembre 1930

Foreboding

Last light wavers   1
between conjoined poplar fingers –
shadow trembles with cold and waiting
behind us
and slowly moves its arms around
to make us more alone –

Last light falls
on the leafage of the limes –
in the sky the poplar fingers
are ringed with stars –   10

Something descends from the sky
toward the trembling shadow –
something passes
into our dark
like a whiteness –
something perhaps that
isn't yet –
someone perhaps who'll be
tomorrow –
a creature perhaps   20
of our sorrow –

Milan, 15th November 1930

La porta che si chiude

Tu lo vedi, sorella: io sono stanca,   1
stanca, logora, scossa,
come il pilastro d'un cancello angusto
al limitare d'un immenso cortile;
come un vecchio pilastro
che per tutta la vita
sia stato diga all'irruente fuga
d'una folla rinchiusa.
Oh, le parole prigioniere
che battono battono   10
furiosamente
alla porta dell'anima
e la porta dell'anima
che a palmo a palmo
spietatamente
si chiude!
Ed ogni giorno il varco si stringe
ed ogni giorno l'assalto è più duro.
E l'ultimo giorno
– io lo so –   20
l'ultimo giorno
quando un'unica lama di luce
pioverà dall'estremo spiraglio
dentro la tenebra,
allora sarà l'onda mostruosa,
l'urto tremendo,
l'urlo mortale
delle parole non nate
verso l'ultimo sogno di sole.
E poi,   30
dietro la porta per sempre chiusa,
sarà la notte intera,

The Closing Door*

You see it, sister: I'm tired,   1
tired, worn out, shaken,
like the column of a strait gate
at the end of a vast courtyard;
like an old column
that all through its life
had been dyke to a headlong flight
of a hemmed-in crowd.
Oh, the imprisoned words
that are beating beating   10
in furious manner
at the door of the spirit
and the door of the spirit
that bit by bit
pitilessly
closes!
And every day the way narrows
and every day the assault is harder.
And the last day
– I know it –   20
on the last day
when a single blade of light
pours from the final loophole
in the shadow,
then it'll be the monstrous wave,
the tremendous crash,
mortal cry
of the unborn words
towards the last dream of sun.
And then,   30
behind the door for ever closed,
there'll be the night entire,

la frescura,
il silenzio.
E poi,
con le labbra serrate,
con gli occhi aperti
sull'arcano cielo dell'ombra,
sarà
— tu lo sai —   40
la pace.

Milano, 10 febbraio 1931

the coolness,
silence.
And then,
with lips sealed,
with eyes open
on the arcane sky of shadow,
there'll be
– you know it –   40
peace.

Milan, 10th February 1931

Nostalgia

C'è una finestra in mezzo alle nubi: 1
potresti affondare
nei cumuli rosa le braccia
e affacciarti
di là
nell'oro.
Chi non ti lascia?
Perché?
Di là c'è tua madre
– lo sai –   10
tua madre col volto proteso
che aspetta il tuo volto.

Kingston, 25 agosto 1931

Nostalgia

There's a window amid the clouds: 1
you might sink your arms
in the pink cumulus
and peep out
over there
in the gold.
Who won't let you?
Why ever?
Beyond there's your mother
– you know –   10
your mother with face forward
waiting for your own face.

Kingston,* 25th August 1931

L'anticamera delle suore

Forse hai ragione tu: 1
forse la pace vera
si può trovare solamente
in un luogo buio come questo,
in un'anticamera di collegio
dove ogni giorno sfilano le bambine
lasciando alle pareti
i soprabitini e i berretti;
dove i poveri vecchi
che vengono a domandare   10
si contentano di un soldo solo
dato da Dio;
dove la sera, per colpa
delle finestre piccine,
si accendono presto le lampade
e non si aspetta
di veder morire la luce,
di veder morire il colore e il rilievo delle cose,
ma incontro alla notte si va
con un proprio lume alto acceso   20
e l'anima che arde non soffre
il disfacimento dell'ombra.

Milano, 12 novembre 1931

The Nuns' Antechamber

Perhaps you're in the right: 1
perhaps true peace
can only be found
in a place dark as this,
in a nunnery antechamber
where girls file daily
leaving on the walls
their little coats and berets;
where poor, aged people
who come to beg for alms   10
are content with one coin only
given them by God;
where at evening, a fault
of the tiny windows,
lamps are lit early
and none wait
to see the light die,
to see the outline and colour of things die
but towards the night you go
with your own lit torch on high   20
and the soul that burns doesn't suffer
the undoing of the shadow.

Milan, 12th November 1931

Prati

Forse non è nemmeno vero   1
quel che a volte ti senti urlare in cuore:
che questa vita è,
dentro il tuo essere,
un nulla
e che ciò che chiamavi la luce
è un abbaglio,
l'abbaglio supremo
dei tuoi occhi malati –
e che ciò che fingevi la meta   10
è un sogno,
il sogno infame
della tua debolezza.

Forse la vita è davvero
quale la scopri nei giorni giovani:
un soffio eterno che cerca
di cielo in cielo
chissà che altezza.

Ma noi siamo come l'erba dei prati
che sente sopra sé passare il vento   20
e tutta canta nel vento
e sempre vive nel vento,
eppure non sa così crescere
da fermare quel volo supremo
né balzare su dalla terra
per annegarsi in lui.

Milano, 31 dicembre 1931

Meadows

Perhaps it isn't even true   1
what at times you hear cry in your heart:
that this life is,
within your being,
a nothing
and what you called light
is a dazzle,
the supreme dazzle
of your sick eyes –
and what you pretended to be the goal   10
is a dream,
the vile dream
of your own weakness.

Perhaps life is really
such as you find it in younger days:
an eternal breath seeking
from sky to sky
who knows what height.

But us, we're like the meadow grass
that above feels the wind pass   20
and all sings in the wind
and forever lives in the wind,
yet can't grow enough
to stop that supreme flight,
or leap up from the earth
and drown in him.

Milan, 31st December 1931

Neve

Turbini di neve   1
che il vento strappa dai tetti
ed altra neve
più quieta
che un'altra mano
arcana
strappa dal cielo –
Turbini di neve fredda sull'anima
e tu non vuoi capire,
tu vuoi sognare   10
triste anima
povera anima
ancora
finché una mano
arcana
strapperà anche il tuo sogno
come un cielo bianco invernale
e in pochi fiocchi nevosi
lo perderà
col vento.   20

10 febbraio 1932

Snow

Whirls of snow   1
wind tears from the roofs
and other snow
more quiet
that another
arcane hand
rips from the sky –
Whirls of snow cold on the soul
and you don't want to understand,
you want to dream   10
sad soul
poor soul
again
until an arcane
hand
will rip your dream too
like a wintry white sky
and in few snowy flakes
will lose it
with the wind.   20

10th February 1932

Tramonto

Fili neri di pioppi –
fili neri di nubi
sul cielo rosso –
e questa prima erba
libera dalla neve
chiara
che fa pensare alla primavera
e guardare
se ad una svolta
nascano le primule –
Ma il ghiaccio inazzurra i sentieri –
la nebbia addormenta i fossati –
un lento pallore devasta
i colori del cielo –
Scende la notte –
nessun fiore è nato –
è inverno – anima –
è inverno.

S. Martino – Milano, 10 gennaio 1933

Sunset*

Black threads of poplars –   1
black threads of clouds
on the red sky –
and this first grass
free from snow
so clear
that it makes you think of spring
and look to see
if at a curve
the primroses blossom –   10
But ice azures the paths –
fog sends ditches to sleep –
a slow pallor wrecks
the sky's colours –
Night's falling –
no flower has bloomed –
it's winter – soul –
it is winter.

S. Martino – Milan, 10th January 1933

In un cimitero di guerra

Così bianca ed intatta è la coltre   1
di neve
su voi
che segnarla del mio passo non oso
dopo tanto cammino
sopra le vie di terra.
Per voi dall'alto suo grembo
di ghiacci e pietra discioglie
un lento manto di nubi
il Cimon della Pala.   10
Per voi taccion le strade
e tace il bosco d'abeti
spegnendo
lungo la valle
ogni volo di vento.
Io strappo alla chioma di un pino
un ramo in forma di croce:
di là dal cancello lo infiggo
per tutte le tombe.
Ma di qua dal cancello   20
serrata
contro le sbarre
dalla mia profonda
pena d'esser viva
rimango
e solo è in pace
con la vostra pace
il sogno
dell'estremo giacere.

(S. Martino) – Milano, 12 gennaio 1933

38

In a War Cemetery

So white and intact is the pall   1
of snow
upon you
I don't dare mark it with my tread
after much walking
over earthy ways.
For you from its high womb
of ice and stone
the Cimon della Pala*
melts a slow mantel of clouds.   10
For you the roads grow silent
and silent the fir-wood
quenching
through the valley
every flight of wind.
I snap from pine foliage
a cruciform branch:
that side of the gate I drive it
through all the tombs.
But this side of the gate   20
pressed up
against the bars
from my deep
pain at being alive
I remain
and only in peace
with your peace
is the dream
of the final repose.

(S. Martino) – Milan, 12th January 1933

39

Luce bianca

All'alba entrai   1
in un piccolo cimitero.

Fu in un paese lontano
ai piedi di una torre grigia
senza più voce alcuna
di campane –
mentre ancora la nebbia
inargentava
le querce oscure,
le siepi alte,   10
l'erica
viola –

Nel piccolo cimitero
le pietre
volte all'Oriente
come in un riso
bianco
parevano visi di ciechi
che allineati marciassero
incontro al sole.   20

1° febbraio 1933

White Light*

At dawn I entered   1
a small graveyard.

It was in a distant country
at a grey tower's foot
without any more voice
of bells at all –
while the fog still
silvered
the dark oaks,
high hedges,   10
the purple
heather –

In the small graveyard
the stones
turned eastward
as in a white
smile
seemed blind men's faces
that marched rank and file
towards the sun.   20

1st February 1933

Sole d'ottobre

Felci grandi   1
e garofani selvaggi
sotto i castani –

mentre il vento scioglie
l'un dopo l'altro
i nodi rossi e biondi
alla veste di foglie
del sole –

e il sole in quella
brucia   10
della sua bianca
bellezza
come un fragile corpo
nudo –

20 ottobre 1933

October Sun

Large ferns   1
and wild pinks
under the chestnuts –

while the wind loosens
one after the other
the red and blond knots
on the leaf-dress
of the sun –

and in there the sun
blazes   10
with its white
beauty
like a fragile
body naked –

20th October 1933

Venezia

Venezia. Silenzio. Il passo   1
di un bimbo scalzo
sulle fondamenta
empie d'echi
il canale.

Venezia. Lentezza. Agli angoli
dei muri sbocciano
alberi e fiori:
come se durasse
un'intera stagione il viaggio,   10
come se maggio
ora
li sdipanasse
per me.

Al pozzo di un campiello
il tempo
trova un filo d'erba tra i sassi:
lega con quello
il suo battito all'ala
di un colombo, al tonfo   20
dei remi.

22 ottobre 1933

Venice

Venice. Silence. The tread 1
of a barefoot boy
on the *fondamenta*
fills the canal
with echoes.

Venice. Slowness. At the corners
of walls there blossom
trees and flowers:
as if the journey
lasted a whole season, 10
as if May-time
now
unravelled them
for me.

At the well in a small square
time
finds a grass blade between stones:
with that it ties
its beat to a pigeon's wing,
to the thudding 20
of the oars.

22nd October 1933

Desiderio di cose leggere

Giuncheto lieve biondo   1
come un campo di spighe
presso il lago celeste

e le case di un'isola lontana
color di vela
pronte a salpare –

Desiderio di cose leggere
nel cuore che pesa
come pietra
dentro una barca –   10

Ma giungerà una sera
a queste rive
l'anima liberata:
senza piegare i giunchi
senza muovere l'acqua o l'aria
salperà – con le case
dell'isola lontana,
per un'alta scogliera
di stelle –

1° febbraio 1934

Desire for Light Things

Blond light rush-bed   1
like a field of wheat
near the sky-blue lake

and the houses on a far island
sail-coloured
ready to set off –

Desire for light things
in the heart that weighs
like stone
inside a boat –   10

But the freed soul one
evening will reach
to these shores:
without bending rushes
without moving water or air
it will set sail – with the distant
island's houses,
for a high cliff face
of stars –

1st February 1934

Nevai

Io fui nel giorno alto che vive   1
oltre gli abeti,
io camminai su campi e monti
di luce –
Traversai laghi morti – ed un segreto
canto mi sussurravano le onde
prigioniere –
passai su bianche rive, chiamando
a nome le genziane
sopite –   10
Io sognai nella neve di un'immensa
città di fiori
sepolta –
io fui sui monti
come un irto fiore –
e guardavo le rocce,
gli alti scogli
per i mari del vento –
e cantavo fra me di una remota
estate, che coi suoi amari   20
rododendri
m'avvampava nel sangue –

1° febbraio 1934

Snowfields

I was in the high day that lives   1
beyond the firs,
I walked on fields and hills
of light –
crossed dead lakes – and imprisoned waves
murmured to me
a secret song –
passed above white banks, calling
by name the drowsy
gentians –   10
I dreamed in the snow
a vast buried city
of flowers –
I was on the mountains
like a bristling flower –
and was looking at rocks,
the high reefs
through seas of wind –
and sang to myself of a distant
summer with its bitter   20
rhododendrons
blazing in my blood –

1st February 1934

Sentiero

È bello camminare lungo il torrente: 1
non si sentono i passi, non sembra
di andare via.
Dall'alto del sentiero si vede la valle
e cime lontane ai margini
della pianura, come pallidi scogli
in riva a una rada – Si pensa
com'è bella, com'è dolce la terra
quando s'attarda a sognare
il tuo tramonto   10
con lunghe ombre azzurre di monti
a lato – Si cammina lungo il torrente:
c'è un gran canto che assorda
la malinconia –

Breil, 9 agosto 1934

Path*

I like to walk by the torrent: 1
you don't hear steps, it doesn't seem
you're going away.
From the path's height you see the valley
and distant peaks at the plain's
margins, like pale reefs
on the shore of a roadstead – You think
how fine, how sweet is the earth
when it lingers to dream,
your sunset   10
with long blue shadows of hills
to the side – you walk by the torrent:
there's a great song deafening
melancholy –

Breil, 9th August 1934

51

Pianura

Certe sere vorrei salire   1
sui campanili della pianura,
veder le grandi nuvole rosa
lente sull'orizzonte
come montagne intessute
di raggi.

Vorrei capire dal cenno dei pioppi
dove passa il fiume
e quale aria trascina;
saper dire dove nascerà il sole   10
domani
e quale via percorrerà, segnata
sul riso già imbiondito,
sui grani.

Vorrei toccare con le mie dita
l'orlo delle campane, quando cade il giorno
e si leva la brezza:
sentir passare nel bronzo il battito
di grandi voli lontani.

n.d.

Plain

Some evenings I'd like to climb
up the bell towers in the plain,
to see the great pink clouds
slow on the horizon
like mountains interwoven
with rays.

I'd understand from poplars' motion
where the river passes
and what wind it drags;
foretell where the sun will rise
tomorrow
and what course it will take, shown
on already whitened rice,
on the grain.

I would touch with my fingers
the rim of the bells, when day declines
and the breeze lifts:
feel pass in their bronze the beat
of great flights far away.

Undated*

Preghiera alla poesia

Oh, tu bene mi pesi   1
l'anima, poesia:
tu sai se io manco e mi perdo,
tu che allora ti neghi
e taci.

Poesia, mi confesso con te
che sei la mia voce profonda:
tu lo sai,
tu lo sai che ho tradito,
ho camminato sul prato d'oro   10
che fu mio cuore,
ho rotto l'erba,
rovinato la terra –
poesia – quella terra
dove tu mi dicesti il più dolce
di tutti i tuoi canti,
dove un mattino per la prima volta
vidi volar nel sereno l'allodola
e con gli occhi cercai di salire –
Poesia, poesia che rimani   20
il mio profondo rimorso,
oh aiutami tu a ritrovare
il mio alto paese abbandonato –
Poesia che ti doni soltanto
a chi con occhi di pianto
si cerca –
oh rifammi tu degna di te,
poesia che mi guardi.

Pasturo, 23 agosto 1934

Prayer to Poetry

Oh, you truly burden   1
my soul, poetry:
you know if I'm failing and lost,
you who then deny yourself
and are silent.

Poetry, I confess to you who are my
deep-down voice:
you know it,
you know I've betrayed,
have walked on the field of gold   10
that was my heart,
I've snapped the grass,
have ruined the ground –
poetry – that ground
where you told me the sweetest
of all your songs,
where one morning for the first time
I saw the lark fly in the clear
and with my eyes I tried to climb –
Poetry, poetry, you that remain   20
my deep down remorse,
oh help me, you, to rediscover
my high abandoned country –
Poetry you that give yourself only
to those who with lamenting eyes
search for themselves –
oh remake me worthy of you,
poetry watching over me.

Pasturo, 23rd August 1934

Odor di verde

Odor di verde –   1
mia infanzia perduta –
quando m'inorgoglivo
dei miei ginocchi segnati –
strappavo inutilmente
i fiori, l'erba in riva ai sentieri,
poi li buttavo –
m'ingombran le mani –

odor di boschi d'agosto – al meriggio –
quando si rompono col viso acceso   10
le ragnatele –
guadando i ruscelli il sasso schizza
il piede affonda
penetra il gelo fin dentro i polsi –
il sole, il sole
sul collo nudo –
la luce che imbiondisce i capelli –

odor di terra,
mia infanzia perduta.

Pasturo, agosto 1934

Scent of Green*

Scent of green –   1
my lost childhood –
when I'd pride myself
on my marked knees –
uselessly I'd pull
flowers, grass beside paths,
then throw them away –
they encumber my hands –

scent of August woods – at midday –
when the spiders' webs   10
are broken with a lit-up face –
fording streams the stone darts
the foot sinks
chill penetrates right to the wrists –
sunshine, sunshine
on my bare neck –
the light bleaching hair –

scent of earth,
my own lost childhood.

Pasturo, August 1934

57

Funerale senza tristezza

Questo non è esser morti,   1
questo è tornare
al paese, alla culla:
chiaro è il giorno
come il sorriso di una madre
che aspettava.
Campi brinati, alberi d'argento, crisantemi
biondi: le bimbe
vestite di bianco,
col velo color della brina,   10
la voce colore dell'acqua
ancora viva
fra terrose prode.
Le fiammelle dei ceri, naufragate
nello splendore del mattino,
dicono quel che sia
questo vanire
delle terrene cose
– dolce –,
questo tornare degli umani,   20
per aerei ponti
di cielo,
per candide creste di monti
sognati,
all'altra riva, ai prati
del sole.

3 dicembre 1934

Funeral with No Sorrow

This isn't being dead,   1
this is coming back
to the village, the cradle:
clear is the day
like the smile of a mother
who'd be waiting.
Frosty fields, silver trees, fair chrysanthemums:
the little girls
dressed in white,
with frost-coloured veil,   10
colour-of-water voices
still living
between earthy banks.
The candle flame-lets, shipwrecked
in morning's brightness
say what it is,
this vanishing
of earthly things
– tender –,
this return of human beings   20
by airy bridges
of sky,
by pure-white crests
of dreamed mountains,
to the other shore, to the meadows
of sun.

3rd December 1934

Confidare

Ho tanta fede in te. Mi sembra   1
che saprei aspettare la tua voce
in silenzio, per secoli
di oscurità.

Tu sai tutti i segreti,
come il sole:
potresti far fiorire
i gerani e la zàgara selvaggia
sul fondo delle cave
di pietra, delle prigioni   10
leggendarie.

Ho tanta fede in te. Son quieta
come l'arabo avvolto
nel barracano bianco,
che ascolta Dio maturargli
l'orzo intorno alla casa.

8 dicembre 1934

Confiding

I've much faith in you. It seems   1
that I could await your voice
in silence, for centuries
of darkness.

You know all the secrets,
like the sun:
you could make flower
geraniums and wild orange blossom
on the rocky depths
of quarries, of the legendary   10
prisons.

I've much faith in you. I'm quiet
like the Arab wrapped
in a white barracan,
who listens to God ripening
his barley round the house.

8th December 1934

Fuochi di S. Antonio

Fiamme nella sera del mio nome   1
sento ardere in riva
a un mare oscuro –
e lungo i porti divampare roghi
di vecchie cose,
d'alghe e di barche
naufragate.

E in me nulla che possa
esser arso,
ma ogni ora di mia vita   10
ancora – con il suo peso indistruttibile
presente –
nel cuore spento della notte
mi segue.

17 gennaio 1935

St Anthony's Fires

Flames in the evening of my name,   1
I feel them burn on the shore
of a dark sea –
and along the ports bonfires
of old things,
algae and shipwrecked
boats catch alight.

And in me nothing that could
be burned,
but every moment of my life   10
still – with its indestructible
weight present –
in the quenched heart of night
follows me.

17th January 1935

Echi

Echi di canti vanno   1
sui pascoli alti,
trecce di falciatrici splendono
nel cielo.

Da lontani orizzonti viene il vento
e scrive parole segrete
su l'erba:
le rimormorano i fiori
tremando nelle lievi
corolle.   10

Echi di canti vanno
sui pascoli alti,
trecce di falciatrici splendono
nel cielo.

26 gennaio 1935

Echoes

Echoes of songs go   1
over high pastures,
braids of mowers sparkle
in the sky.

From far horizons comes the wind
and writes secret words
over grass:
the flowers murmur them again
trembling in their delicate
corollas.   10

Echoes of songs go
over high pastures,
braids of mowers sparkle
in the sky.

26th January 1935

Atene

Con l'alba   1
dal mare salivo
per alte scalee: si piegavano
cieli d'attesa ai margini
della pietra.

E traboccò per la spianata il sole.

Tepidi fiotti corsero nei fusti
delle colonne,
dense vene si aprirono
di linfa bionda: 10

si levarono i templi nella luce
come mani vive

e misuravo tra le aeree dita
gli spazi
di un eterno mattino.

(20 aprile 1934) 28 gennaio 1935

Athens*

With the dawn   1
from sea I'd climb
by high stairs: awaiting skies
bent down at the margins
of the stone.

And sun brimmed over the plain.

Warm gushes ran in the shafts
of the columns,
dense veins opened
with blond lymph: 10

temples lifted in the light
like living hands

and I'd measure through airy fingers
the spaces
of an eternal morning.

(20th April 1934) 28th January 1935

Africa

Terra,   1
sei di chi affonda
nella sabbia le mani,
in un'esigua conca
pianta un ulivo.

Non hai strade: misuri
il tempo del cammino
con la distanza dei pozzi,
cippi sono
le bianche tombe dei tuoi santi   10
nel deserto.

Non hai bàratri: proteso
è il tuo colore biondo
senza confini.
Abbeverate di cammelli chiamano
lembi di cielo
sul tuo volto scoperto.

Cielo
che dilati le stelle,
vento – che imbianchi   20
d'eucalipti le sere,

o terra,
cielo vento –
libertà
di sogni.

28 gennaio 1935

Africa

Earth, 1
you are his who sinks
hands into the sand,
plants an olive
in a little hollow.

You don't have roads: you measure
the walking time
with the distance between wells,
milestones
are white tombs of your saints 10
in the desert.

You don't have abysses: outspread
is your blond colour
without boundaries.
Camels' watering places call
strips of sky
onto your uncovered face.

Sky
how you dilate the stars,
wind – how you whiten 20
evenings with eucalyptuses,

O earth,
sky wind –
liberty
of dreams.

28th January 1935

Un destino

Lumi e capanne   1
ai bivi
chiamarono i compagni.

A te resta
questa che il vento ti disvela
pallida strada nella notte:
alla tua sete
la precipite acqua dei torrenti,
alla persona stanca
l'erba dei pascoli che si rinnova 10
nello spazio di un sonno.

In un suo fuoco assorto
ciascuno degli umani
ad un'unica vita si abbandona.

Ma sul lento
tuo andar di fiume che non trova foce,
l'argenteo lume di infinite
vite – delle libere stelle
ora trema:
e se nessuna porta   20
s'apre alla tua fatica,
se ridato
t'è ad ogni passo il peso del tuo volto,
se è tua
questa che è più di un dolore
gioia di continuare sola
nel limpido deserto dei tuoi monti

ora accetti
d'esser poeta.

13 febbraio 1935

A Fate*

Gleams and shelters   1
where roads divide
called to the companions.

To you remains
this that the wind unveils for you,
pale road in the night:
for your thirst
the tumbling torrents' water,
for someone tired
the pasture grass renewed   10
in the space of a sleep.

Absorbed in his own fire
everyone human
surrenders to a single life.

But on your slow
going as a river that finds no end,
the silvery light of infinite
lives – of the free stars
trembles now:
and if not one door   20
opens to your weariness,
if it's rebuffed
at every step your face's burden,
if it is yours
this that's more than pain,
joy of going on alone
in the clear desert of your hills

now you accept
you're a poet.

13th February 1935

Radio

Usignolo in altissime fronde   1
dietro l'occhio rossastro
cantò:
da buie grotte d'aria
aggrumandosi gli echi,
note
nel cavo della stanza
stillarono.

Uno scalpiccìo folto ci parlò
d'invisibili lumi,   10
della vita
che s'annoda a singulti di sassofono,
poi gli occhi apre
ridesta
fra due battiti di palme.

E di nuovo cantò
l'usignolo
in altissime fronde, dal Maggio
di paesi esiliati:
evasa un'onda   20
di voci
dagli oceani della sera
irruppe a questo scoglio di silenzio.

15 maggio 1935

Radio

Nightingale in highest fronds   1
behind the reddish eye
it sang:
from dark caves of air
as echoes curdling,
notes
dripped in the room's
hollow.

A thick shuffle spoke to us
of invisible lights,   10
of life
that's tied to saxophone sobs,
then the eyes it opens
reawakened
between two beats of palms.

And once more it sang,
the nightingale
in highest fronds, from the May
of exiled countries:
escaped, a wave   20
of voices
from the evening's oceans
it burst upon this reef of silence.

15th May 1935

Tempo

Mentre tu dormi   1
le stagioni passano
sulla montagna.

La neve in alto
struggendosi dà vita
al vento:
dietro la casa il prato parla,
la luce
beve orme di pioggia sui sentieri.

Mentre tu dormi   10
anni di sole passano
fra le cime dei làrici
e le nubi.

28 maggio 1935

II

Io posso cogliere i mughetti
mentre tu dormi
perché so dove crescono.
E la mia vera casa
con le sue porte e le sue pietre
sia lontana,
né io più la ritrovi,   20
ma vada errando
pei boschi
eternamente –
mentre tu dormi
ed i mughetti crescono
senza tregua.

28 maggio 1935

Time

While you sleep   1
the seasons pass
on the mountain.

The snow up high
wearing thin gives life
to the wind:
behind the house the meadow speaks,
the light
drinks prints of rain on the paths.

While you sleep   10
years of sun pass
between the larches' tops
and the clouds.

28th May 1935

II

I can gather lilies of the valley
while you sleep
as I know where they grow.
And my true home
with its doors and stones
be far away,
nor I ever regain it,   20
but wander astray
through woods
eternally –
while you sleep
and the lilies of the valley grow
without respite.

28th May 1935

75

Precoce autunno

La nebbia è d'argento, cancella   1
le ombre dei pini:
sono più grandi i giardini
nell'alba.

Al pioppo una foglia è ingiallita,
un ramo è morto al castano
sul monte.

Spaventi che non sanno se stessi
dormendo nell'aria celeste:
questa fine che torna ogni anno,   10
che è nuova ogni anno.

Come l'ultimo albero del bosco,
l'ultimo uomo ha contato le morti:
pur la sua morte lo coglie
ancora stupito.

18 agosto 1935

Premature Autumn

Fog is silvery, it deletes
the pines' shadows:
gardens are larger
in dawn light.

For the poplar a leaf is yellowed,
a bough's dead in the chestnut
on the hill.

Fears that don't know themselves
sleeping in blue air:
this end that returns each year
and each year's new.

Like the last tree in the wood,
the last man's counted the dead:
yet his own death takes him
unawares still.

18th August 1935

Le donne

In urlo di sirene   1
una squadriglia
fiammante spezza il cielo.

Rotte tra case affondano
le campane.

S'affacciano le donne
a tricolori abbracciate;
gridan coraggio
nel vento
i loro biondi capelli.   10

Poi,
occhi si chinano spenti.

Nella sera
guardan laggiù il primo morto
disteso sotto le stelle.

3 ottobre 1935

The Women*

In siren howl   1
a flaming
squadron splits the sky.

Broken between houses
the bells sink down.

The women appear
tricolour flags in arms;
it cries courage
in the wind,
their blonde hair.   10

Then,
spent eyes lower.

In the evening
they look down there on the first dead
stretched out under the stars.

3rd October 1935

Spazioso autunno

Or che i violini   1
hanno cessato di suonare

ed una foglia volteggiando
sfiora
il braccio bianco di Venere
in fondo al viale

andiamo per la brughiera
a veder nascere le stelle:

sono i visi delle ginestre morte.

Ora infuriano i cavalli nella stalla: 10
ma vagano lassù
con le nubi
le ombre delle lor lunghe criniere
rosse.

Inseguiamo fitte orme di zoccoli.

Ed è pieno di ali e di chiome
invisibili
quest'aperto campo notturno.

23 dicembre 1935

Spacious Autumn

Now that the violins   1
have stopped sounding

and a turning leaf
grazes
the white arm of Venus
at the avenue's end

we go across the moor
to see stars appear:

they're the faces of dead broom.

Now in the stall the horses rage: 10
but there wander above
with the clouds
the shadows of their long
red manes.

We're following packed-close hoof prints.

And it is full of invisible
wings and plumes
this open night-time field.

23rd December 1935

Approdo

Fruscìo sordo di legni 1
sovra il lago
sepolto:

ci scompare
alle spalle in un turbine di neve
la pista esile dritta.

Ora si leva
la voce di un attacco nel passo.

Stride ritmico:
e forse è freddo pianto di bivacchi, 10
grido di spaventevoli bufere;
o è lamento d'uccelli,
ansito roco
di volpi gracili vedute morire –

Non andiamo ai confini di una terra?
E quando in altre vesti
alle calde vetrate sosterò –
(la slitta
m'avrà rapita
nel giro dei suoi campanelli, 20
avrò alle spalle
lampade volti canti) –

la mia ombra
sarà sul lago,
pegno immoto di me
fuori – alla triste
favolosa sera.

Misurina, 12 gennaio 1936

Landing

Mute rustle of wood   1
above the
buried lake:

it disappears
behind us in a whirl of snow,
the thin straight track.

Now there rises
the voice of an attack in the pass.

Rhythmic it shrieks:
and perhaps it's bivouacs' cold complaint,   10
cry of fearful storms;
or it's birds' lament,
hoarse gasp
of frail foxes seen to die –

Shan't we go to the edges of a land?
And when in other clothes
at the hot glass panes I'll rest –
(the sledge
will have stolen me off
in the spin of its bells,   20
I'll have at my back
lamps, faces, songs) –

my shadow
will be on the lake
still pledge of me
outside – in the sad
fabulous evening.

Misurina, 12th January 1936

Rifugio

Mentre di fuori il sole sgela   1
pelli di foca
ai cardini dell'uscio

scostate queste tazze di vin caldo
e il pane sbriciolato,
fate posto:
ora voglio dormire.

Se ridi
e scuoti il ciuffo del mio berretto rosso
come a un bambino insonnolito,   10
io cado
in golfi oscuri e caldi
di sogno.

Ma perché
una canzone marinaresca
fra strapiombi neri?

Dimmi che non possiamo
andare oltre:
questa pista finisce alla forcella,
alta e intatta è la neve   20
sul versante
dell'ombra.

Qui crediamo
eterna luce sovra campi splendenti:
potrà mai
venir sera ai nostri vetri
d'argento?

Refuge

While outside the sun unfreezes   1
sealskins on
the door hinges

put aside these cups of *vin brulé*
and the crumbled bread,
make space:
now I want to sleep.

If you laugh
and shake my red beret tuft
as with a drowsy child,   10
me I fall
into dark and warm gulfs
of dreaming.

But why
a sailor's shanty
among black precipices?

Tell me we cannot
go beyond:
this track ends at the pass,
high and virgin is the snow   20
on the slope
of shadow.

Here we believe
eternal light above shining fields:
could evening ever
come to our windows'
silver?

III

Noi,
quando grigie fascie di tormenta
strapperanno da terra   30
il nostro rosso
nido di pietra,
guarderemo nudi –
come da un celeste
Walhalla –
i laghi spenti in fondo ai pini,
le fioche
lampade erranti dei pastori.

19 gennaio 1936

III

We,
when grey strips of blizzard
will tear from earth   30
our red
nest of stone,
we'll look out bare –
as from a sky-blue
Valhalla –
at dull lakes down in the pines,
the faint
wandering lamps of the shepherds.

19th January 1936

Periferia

Lampi di brace nella sera: 1
e stridono
due sigarette spente in una pozza.

Fra lame d'acqua buia
non ha echi
il tuo ridere rosso:
apre misteri
di primitiva umanità.

Fra poco
urlerà la sirena della fabbrica: 10
curvi profili in corsa
schiuderanno
laceri varchi nella nebbia.

Oscure
masse di travi: e il peso
del silenzio tra case non finite
grava con noi
sulla fanghiglia,
ai piedi
dell'ultimo fanale.   20

19 gennaio 1936

Outskirts

Glows of embers in the evening: 1
and two cigarettes
shriek extinguished in a puddle.

Between blades of dark water
your red laugh
has no echoes:
it opens secrets
of primitive humanity.

In a while
the factory siren will howl: 10
hurrying bent profiles
will reveal
ragged passages in the fog.

Dark masses
of beams: and amongst unfinished
houses the burden of silence
weighs with us
on slush
at the final
lamp post's foot.   20

19th January 1936

Portofino

Lontani dai mandorli vivi   1
hanno piccole tombe
infisse agli scogli
i bambini: a tonfi percossa
nel cavo cuore selvaggio,
d'alghe avvinta
la roccia, in anelli di vertigine.

Ma lenta disfà la penisola
i suoi nodi di terra,
spiega in vetta   10
vele d'oscure foreste:

all'infinita
altalena degli orizzonti
già china,

offrendo
i suoi lievi sepolcri
ai bracci di una gran croce lunare.

aprile 1936

Portofino*

Far from the living almond trees   1
they have little tombs
cut into the cliffs
the children: beaten with thuds
in its hollow wild heart,
the rock gripped
by algae, in vertigo rings.

But the peninsula slowly undoes
its knots of earth,
unfurls up above   10
sails of dark forests:

at the infinite
see-saw of the horizons
already bowed,

offering
its light sepulchres
to the arms of a great lunar cross.

April 1936

Viaggio al nord

Primavera che ci dolevi   1
oltre il valico,
ora riaffonda
nostra ansia serale per la piana:
i nostri fiori
son fari rossi e verdi
alle folate di tormenta, l'albero
di nostra vita si biforca agli scambi.

Primavera che più non duoli,
t'uccide   10
tra lumi or sottilissima la neve
e il vin dolce ti smemora
terra perduta:
ma ai muri
corolle enormi di giunchiglie fingono
un mondo di miracoli
per gli insetti...

Ripudia
questo sangue il suo sole e le stagioni
infuriando   20
così sotterra, nella magica notte.

Berlino, febbraio–marzo 1937

Journey to the North

Spring how you pained us   1
beyond the pass,
now through the plain
our evening disquiet sinks again:
our flowers
are red and green headlights
at the torment's gusts, the tree
of our life's split at the points.

Spring how you pain us no more,
it kills you   10
the now thinnest snow amid lights
and the sweet wine makes you forget
lost earth:
but at the walls
vast corollas of daffodils feign
a world of miracles
for the insects...

This blood
rejects its sun and the seasons
raging so   20
below ground, in the magical night.

Berlin, February–March 1937

Periferia in aprile

Intorno aiole   1
dove ragazzo t'affannavi al calcio:
ed or fra cocci
s'apron fiori terrosi al secco fiato
dei muri a primavera.
Ma nella voce e nello sguardo
hai acqua,
tu profonda frescura, radicata
oltre le zolle e le stagioni, in quella
che ancor resta alle cime   10
umida neve:
così correndo in ogni vena
e dici
ancora quella strada remotissima
ed il vento
leggero sopra enormi
baratri azzurri.

24 aprile 1937

Outskirts in April

Around flower beds   1
where a boy you'd get breathless at football:
and now among shards
earthy flowers open at the dry breath
of the walls come spring.
But in your voice and gaze
there's water,
you deep freshness, rooted
beyond the clods and seasons, in what
on the peaks remains still   10
wet snow:
thus running in every vein
and you say
again that furthest road
and the wind
light above vast
azure chasms.

24th April 1937

Brughiera

I

Accoccolato tra le pervinche   1
sfuggi
la furia ansante dei cavalli
e l'urlo
dei cani al sole.

Tu sei come il ramarro verde e azzurro
che del proprio rumore si spaura
e hai cari
questi ciliegi appena in fiore, quasi
senz'ombra.   10

Tenui
profili di colline alle tue ciglia:
e all'orecchio
così curvo sull'erica riarsa
a quando a quando il rombo
dei puledri lanciati per la piana.

Con le farfalle raso terra
esitavi
al fiorire della ginestra:
e ad un tratto   20
enormi ali ti dà
quest'ombra trasvolante in rombo.

Ora ridi,
acciaio splendido,
all'ombroso
imbizzarrirsi dei cavalli, al pavido
balzare delle lepri fra i narcisi.

Heathland

I

Crouched amid the periwinkles   1
you flee
the horses' panting fury
and the cry
of dogs in sunlight.

You're like the blue-and-green lizard
scared by its own sound
and you hold dear
these barely blossomed cherry trees, almost
with no shadow.   10

Faint profiles
of hills on your eyebrows
and at the ear
so bent on the parched heather
every now and then a rumble
of colts loosed over the plain.

II

With the butterflies grazing earth
you'd hesitate
at the flowering of the broom:
and suddenly   20
it gives you vast wings
this shadow flying by in a roar.

Now you laugh,
splendid steel,
at the shadowy
shying of horses, the fearful
jumping of hares through narcissi.

Indugiano
carezze non date
fra le dita dei peschi   30
e gli sguardi
d'amore che mai non avemmo
s'appendono alle glicini sui ponti –

Ma il fiume
è densa furia d'acque senza creste, nel grembo
porta profondi visi di montagne:
e all'immenso
svolto dei boschi trova lieve il vento,
tocca le fresche nuvole
d'aprile.   40

28 aprile 1937

III

They linger
caresses not given
between peach-tree fingers   30
and the looks
of love we never had
hung from wisteria on bridges –

But the river's
a thick fury of crestless waters, in its lap
it bears deep faces of mountains:
and at the vast
turning of woods it finds the soft wind,
touches the fresh clouds
of April.   40

28th April 1937

Sete

Or vuoi ch'io ti racconti   1
una storia di pesci
mentre il lago s'annebbia?
Ma non vedi
come batte la sete nella gola
delle lucertole sul fogliame trito?
A terra
i ricci morti d'autunno
hanno trafitto le pervinche.
E mordi   10
gli steli arsi: ti sanguina
già lievemente l'angolo del labbro.
Ed or vuoi
ch'io ti racconti una storia d'uccelli?
Ma all'afa
del mezzogiorno il cuculo feroce
svolazza solo.
Ed ancora
urla tra i rovi il cucciolo perduto:
forse il baio in corsa   20
con lo zoccolo nero lo colpì
sul muso.

28 aprile 1937

Thirst*

Do you want me to tell you   1
a story of fish now
while the lake fogs over?
But don't you see
how thirst strikes in the throat
of lizards on worn foliage?
On the ground
autumn's dead husks
have transfixed the periwinkles.
And you bite   10
the parched stalks: already
bleed a touch at your lip corner.
And now you want
me to tell you a story of birds?
But in the heat
at midday the ferocious cuckoo
flaps about alone.
And again
among brambles the lost puppy howls:
perhaps the running bay horse   20
struck it with its black hoof
on the face.

28th April 1937

Treni

A notte   1
un lento giro d'ombre rosse
alle pareti avviava i treni: tonfi
cupi d'agganci
al sonno si frangevano.

E lavava
lieve la corsa della pioggia il fumo
denso ai cristalli: sogni
s'aprivano continui, balenanti
binari lungo un fiume.   10

Ora ritorna
a volte a mezzo il sonno quel tuonare
assurdo
e per le mute vie serali, ai lenti
legni dei carri e dentro il sangue
chiama
lunghi fragori – e quell'antico ardente
spavento e sogno
di convogli.

Torino, 1° maggio 1937

Trains

At night   1
a slow turning of red shadows
on walls set going the trains: dark
thuds of couplings
were breaking over sleep.

And the rain's course
lightly washed the dense smoke
on windows: dreams
were forever opening, flashing
tracks beside a river.   10

Now that absurd
thunder returns at times in the midst
of sleep
and through still evening streets, to the slow
wood of carts and within the blood
it calls up
long clangs – and that old burning
fear and dream
of convoys.

Turin, 1st May 1937

Fine di una domenica

Rotta da un fischio   1
all'ultimo tumulto
s'è scomposta la mischia: sulle lacere
maglie e sui volti in furia – vedo
il cielo dello stadio bianco, quasi
soffice lana.

Calmi greggi dormono
a fronte d'alte case,
in rozze strade
dilaganti per l'erba: e non ha un senso   10
quest'avviarsi di treni verso incerte
pianure...

Ormai il fiume
è un lago fermo tra muraglie, in fondo
ad un bosco serale: lenti viali
in cerchio ci trascinano – ove imbarca
coppie d'amanti la corrente...

E a noi
forse sovviene di un istante, quando
qualche cosa si perse   20
ad un crocicchio:
che non sappiamo.
Sì che vuote
ora – e disgiunte
senza amore ci pendono le mani.

Torino, 2 maggio 1937

A Sunday's End

Broken by a whistle   1
at the final tumult
the byplay's dissolved: on the torn
jerseys and angry faces – I see
the white stadium's sky, almost
soft wool.

Calm flocks sleep
before high houses,
in rough streets
spreading through grass: and it has no sense   10
this setting off of trains towards uncertain
plateaus...

By now the river
is a still lake between great walls, in the deep
of an evening wood: slow avenues
in a ring draw us on – where couples
of lovers embark on the current...

And to us
an instant perhaps comes back, when
something was lost   20
at a crossroads:
which we don't know.
So that empty
now – detached
without love our hands hang down.

Turin, 2nd May 1937

Sonno e risveglio sulla terra

A mezzogiorno si sfiancò il galoppo   1
dei puledri sui prati.
Tu guardavi
inalberarsi ai làrici i cavalli
sauri del sole:
così prona tra ciuffi di ginestra –
e in lunghi istanti
poi sparivi alla terra.

Fondo nodo
di una radice: e fu muta magìa   10
quando cani lentissimi ti sorsero
a fronte nel crepuscolo –
grandi e giovani, bianchi e neri –
e apristi lene fiamma
d'umiltà
nei loro occhi
castani.

Ora si torce
acre tra i rovi la tua voglia gracile
della vita: e sei giglio   20
improvviso sul bordo di una forra
quando fresca nel vento
ti solleva
la tua rossa brughiera.

11 maggio 1937

Sleep and Waking on Earth

At midday the colts' gallop dispersed   1
over meadows.
You were watching
sorrel horses of sunlight hoist themselves
into the larches:
lain like this between broom tufts –
and for long moments
then you disappeared to earth.

Profound knot
of a root: and it was mute witchcraft   10
when dogs so slowly rose
before you in the dusk –
large and young, white and black –
and opened humility's
tender flame
in their eyes
of chestnut brown.

Now it writhes
bitter between brambles your frail
will in life: and you're suddenly   20
lily on a gorge's edge
when fresh in the wind
it uplifts you
your red moorland.

11th May 1937

Bambino morente

In una notte hai vissuto   1
gli anni di tutta la vita:
e l'alba lenta te ne incorona
come di spine. Guardi
con savi occhi le ombre
intorno brancolanti, incompiute:
e sai la pena del grano riverso fra i tuoni
e i vuoti nelle mandrie insidiate.
In mille sere
ravviasti lunghe trecce grige, ti oppresse   10
l'umidore dei giorni sfioriti;
ora s'apre
in un filo di sole la tua fronte, si spiana
nello sguardo di un uomo perfetto:
e compiangi tua madre.

10 giugno 1937

Dying Child

In a night you've lived   1
a whole life's years:
and slow dawn crowns you
with them like thorns. You look
from wise eyes at shadows
groping around, incomplete:
and know the ache of wheat bent through thunder
and gaps in the threatened herd.
In a thousand evenings
you've tidied long grey tresses, oppressed   10
by the damp of withered days;
now your forehead
opens in a beam of sun, is smoothed
in the gaze of a perfect man:
and you mourn for your mother.

10th June 1937

I morti

Siedon sul grembo dei prati   1
a un crocicchio di strade:
odon fruscìo di ruote per la china,
bimbi e cavalli saltare le siepi.

Sentono il tuono venire,
gli scrosci sul nudo fieno
(quando gli uomini per salvarlo
escono dalle case
coi corpi protesi alla terra).

Ogni sera,   10
prima che il campanile verde sbocci in suono,
si domandan se la cresta del monte
non disegni un bambino riverso
dormente su loro.

Poi, quando nel cavo degli occhi
corolle sperse di campane
scendono a bere,
lenti essi volgono il volto
ai cancelli:
se d'autunno un pastore s'attardi   20
senza timore a rompere il suo pane
e il gregge chiaro si prema alle sbarre.

Allora ridono i morti
piano fra loro:
sognano lieve e più calda la notte.

Pasturo, 8 settembre 1937

The Dead

They sit in the fields' lap   1
at a meeting of roads:
hear wheels' rustle on the slope,
kids and horses jumping hedges.

They hear thunder coming,
the cloudbursts on bare hay
(when to save it men
come from the houses
with bodies outstretched on the earth).

Every evening,   10
before the green bell tower flow with sound,
they wonder if the hill crest
doesn't outline a child lain down
sleeping upon them.*

Then, when into their eye sockets
scattered corollas of bells
go down to drink,
slowly they turn faces
to the gates:
if a shepherd linger in autumn   20
fearless to break his bread
and the clear flock press at the bars.

Well then the dead laugh quietly
between themselves:
they dream the night's lighter and warmer.

Pasturo, 8th September 1937

Le montagne

Occupano come immense donne   1
la sera:
sul petto raccolte le mani di pietra
fissan sbocchi di strade, tacendo
l'infinita speranza di un ritorno.

Mute in grembo maturano figli
all'assente. (Lo chiamaron vele
laggiù – o battaglie. Indi azzurra e rossa
parve loro la terra). Ora a un franare
di passi sulle ghiaie   10
grandi trasalgon nelle spalle. Il cielo
batte in un sussulto le sue ciglia bianche.

Madri. E s'erigon nella fronte, scostano
dai vasti occhi i rami delle stelle:
se all'orlo estremo dell'attesa
nasca un'aurora

e al brullo ventre fiorisca rosai.

Pasturo, 9 settembre 1937

The Mountains

Like vast women they occupy   1
the evening:
stone hands folded on their breast
they gaze on road ends, silencing
the infinite hope of return.

Speechless in the womb mature
children to the absent. (Sails called him
down there – or battles. So earth seemed
blue and red to them). Now at a slippage
of steps on the pebbles   10
immense they shudder their shoulders. The sky
with a start beats its white eyelids.

Mothers. And they raise their foreheads, shift
the branches of stars from large eyes:
should at the last rim of waiting
an aurora be born

and at the bare belly rose bushes bloom.

Pasturo, 9th September 1937

Sera a settembre

Aria di neve ai monti   I
ora colmi il villaggio di campani,
porte spalanchi al magro
ultimo fieno:

quando ai carri s'aggrappano bambini
e affioran rade, calde per la valle
trasparenze di case illuminate.

Dall'ombra – allora – a me salgono nenie
di zingari accampati sulle strade…

Pasturo, 13 settembre 1937

September Evening

Air of snow in the mountains I
now you fill the village with bells,
throw open doors on
the last thin hay:

when children catch hold of carts
and down the valley surface sparse, warm
transparencies of lights in the houses.

From the shadow – then – to me climb dirges
of Gypsies camped upon the roads…

Pasturo, 13th September 1937

Voce di donna

Io nacqui sposa di te soldato.   1
So che a marce e a guerre
lunghe stagioni ti divelgon da me.

Curva sul focolare aduno bragi,
sopra il tuo letto ho disteso un vessillo –
ma se ti penso all'addiaccio
piove sul mio corpo autunnale
come su un bosco tagliato.

Quando balena il cielo di settembre
e pare un'arma gigantesca sui monti,   10
salvie rosse mi sbocciano sul cuore;
Che tu mi chiami,
che tu mi usi
con la fiducia che dai alle cose,
come acqua che versi sulle mani
o lana che ti avvolgi intorno al petto.

Sono la scarna siepe del tuo orto
che sta muta a fiorire
sotto convogli di zingare stelle.

18 settembre 1937

116

Woman's Voice

I was born bride to you soldier,   1
know that to marches and wars
long seasons uproot you from me.

Bent over the hearth I rake embers,
on your bed I've spread a banner –
but if I think of you at the bivouac
it rains on my autumnal body
as onto a cut-down wood.

When the September sky flashes
and it seems a giant weapon on the hills,   10
red sages blossom on my heart;
How you call me,
how you use me
with the trust you give things,
like water you pour on your hands
or wool you wrap round your breast.

I'm the bare hedge to your garden
staying mute to flower
under convoys of Gypsy stars.

18th September 1937

Morte di una stagione

Piovve tutta la notte   1
sulle memorie dell'estate.

A buio uscimmo
entro un tuonare lugubre di pietre,
fermi sull'argine reggemmo lanterne
a esplorare il pericolo dei ponti.

All'alba pallidi vedemmo le rondini
sui fili fradice immote
spiare cenni arcani di partenza –

e le specchiavano sulla terra   10
le fontane dai volti disfatti.

Pasturo, 20 settembre 1937

Death of a Season

It rained all night   1
on the memories of summer.

At dark we went out
amidst a funereal thunder of stones,
still on the banks we held lanterns
to explore the bridges' danger.

Pale at dawn we saw swallows
drenched on the wires poised
to spy out arcane signs of departure –

and they were mirrored on earth   10
by the fountains from faces undone.

Pasturo, 20th September 1937

La terra

Stella morta, ai tuoi orli   I
nubi di sogno e corolle di parole
volgi nei cieli.

Vedo per fondi mari
pescatori notturni metter barche
e sulle chiglie tracciare ghirlande
di gialle margherite,

vedo in fronte ai ghiacci
volti di santi spalancarsi all'alba
sui muri delle stalle: 10

e a mezzodì s'avanza il vecchio gobbo,
canta sui ciotoli e per le donne accorse
fra i trilli del suo timpano d'argento:
«È fiorito il bambù, dopo cent'anni.
In riva a tutti i mari e ne morrà.
Coll'autunno si secca la foglia,
a oriente scorron fossati di sangue,
vidi le braccia di migliaia d'uccisi
penzolar sull'abisso
ad occidente.»   20

Nubi di pianto e corolle di deliri
si torcono ai tuoi orli
o Terra.

1° novembre 1937

The Earth

Dead star, at your brims   1
dream clouds and word corollas
revolve in the skies.

I see through deep seas
night fishermen put out boats
and on bows trail garlands
of yellow marguerites,

I see before glaciers
saints' faces flung open at dawn
on the stable walls: 10

and at midday the old hunchback nears,
sings on the cobbles for hastening women
through his silver tambourine trills:
"Bamboo's flowered, after a hundred years.
On all the seas' shores and it will die.
With autumn the leaf shrivels,
to the east flow ditches of blood,
I saw the arms of thousands killed
hanging on the abyss
to the west."   20

Grief clouds and frenzy corollas
writhe at your brims
O Earth.

1st November 1937

Nebbia

Se c'incontrassimo questa sera   1
pel viale oppresso di nebbia
si asciugherebbero le pozzanghere
intorno al nostro scoglio caldo di terra:
e la mia guancia sopra le tue vesti
sarebbe dolce salvezza della vita.
Ma fronti lisce di fanciulle
a me rimproverano gli anni: un albero
solo ho compagno nella tenebra piovosa
e lumi lenti di carri mi fanno temere,   10
temere e chiamare la morte.

27 novembre 1937

Fog

If we were to meet this evening   1
on the avenue oppressed with fog
the puddles would dry
round our warm reef of earth:
and my cheek above your clothes
would be life's sweet salvation.
But smooth foreheads of young girls
reproach me for the years: a tree's
my one companion in the rainy dark
and slow lights of trucks make me fear,   10
fear and call for death.

27th November 1937

Capodanno

Se le parole sapessero di neve   I
stasera, che canti –
e le stelle
che non potrò mai dire…

Volti immoti s'intrecciano fra i rami
nel mio turchino nero:
osano ancora,
morti ai lumi di case lontane,
l'indistrutto sorriso dei miei anni.

Madonna di Campiglio,
31 dicembre 1937–1° gennaio 1938

New Year

If the words tasted of snow   I
this evening, what songs –
and the stars
that I'll never be able to say…

Still faces intertwine through branches
in my turquoise black:
again they dare,
dead in the lights of far houses,
the un-ruined smile of my years.*

Madonna di Campiglio,
31st December 1937–1st January 1938

Certezza

Tu sei l'erba e la terra, il senso   1
quando uno cammina a piedi scalzi
per un campo arato.
Per te annodavo il mio grembiule rosso
e ora piego a questa fontana
muta immersa in un grembo di monti:
so che a un tratto
– il mezzogiorno sciamerà coi gridi
dei suoi fringuelli –
sgorgherà il tuo volto   10
nello specchio sereno, accanto al mio.

9 gennaio 1938

Certainty

You're the grass and earth, the sense   1
when one walks barefoot
across a ploughed field.
For you I'd tie my red apron on
and bend now at this mute
fountain immersed in a womb of hills:
I know that suddenly
– midday will swarm with the cries
of its finches –
will spring forth your face   10
in the calm mirror, beside mine.

9th January 1938

Periferia

Sento l'antico spasimo   1
– è la terra
che sotto coperte di gelo
solleva le sue braccia nere –
e ho paura
dei tuoi passi fangosi, cara vita,
che mi cammini a fianco, mi conduci
vicino a vecchi dai lunghi mantelli,
a ragazzi
veloci in groppa a opache biciclette,   10
a donne,
che nello scialle si premono i seni –

E già sentiamo
a bordo di betulle spaesate
il fumo dei comignoli morire
roseo sui pantani.

Nel tramonto le fabbriche incendiate
ululano per il cupo avvio dei treni…

Ma pezzo muto di carne io ti seguo
e ho paura –   20
pezzo di carne che la primavera
percorre con ridenti dolori.

21 gennaio 1938

Outskirts

I sense the old pang   1
– it's the earth
under covers of ice
raising its black arms –
and I'm afraid
of your muddy steps, dear life,
that walk beside me, lead me
near to old men with long cloaks,
to quick boys
astride opaque bikes,   10
to women,
who press breasts in their shawls –

And we sense already
alongside displaced birch trees
the smoke of chimneys die
pinkish on the mires.

In the sunset enflamed factories
howl for the gloomy start of trains...

But mute piece of flesh I follow you
and am afraid –   20
piece of flesh the springtime
runs through with smiling sorrows.

21st January 1938

Luci libere

1
È un sole bianco che intenerisce
sui monumenti le donne di bronzo.

Vorresti sparire alle case, destarti
ove trascinano lenti carri
sbarre di ferro verso la campagna –

ché là pei fossi infuriano bambini
nell'acqua, all'aurora
e vi crollano immagini di pioppi.

Noi, per seguir la danza
di un vecchio organo   10
correremmo nel vento gli stradali...

A cuore scalzo
e con laceri pesi
di gioia.

27 gennaio 1938

Free Lights

It's a white sun makes tender   1
women of bronze on the monuments.

You'd like to disappear in the houses, awake
where slow carts drag
iron rods towards the countryside –

since there along ditches kids rage
in the water, at dawn
and images of poplars topple there.

We, to follow the dance
of an old organ   10
we'd run in the wind down lanes…

With barefoot heart
and torn burdens
of joy.

27th January 1938

Pan

Mi danzava una macchia di sole   1
tepida sulla fronte,
c'era ancora un frusciare di vento
tra foglie lontanissime.

Poi venne
solo: la schiuma di queste onde di sangue
e un martellio di campane nel buio,
giù nel buio per vortici intensi,
per rossi colpi di silenzio – allo schianto.

Dopo   10
riallacciavano le formiche
nere fila di vita tra l'erba
vicino ai capelli
e sul mio – sul tuo volto sudato
una farfalla batteva le ali.

27 febbraio 1938

Pan

A stain of sun danced for me   1
lukewarm on my brow,
there was a rustle of wind again
through remotest leaves.

Then on his own
he came: the foam of these blood waves
and a bells' hammering in darkness,
down in the dark through intense swirls,
through red blows of silence – at the crashing.

Later   10
the ants would stitch black lines
of life through the grass
near to the hair
and on your sweaty face – on mine
a butterfly beat its wings.

27th February 1938

Via dei Cinquecento

Pesano fra noi due   1
troppe parole non dette

e la fame non appagata,
gli urli dei bimbi non placati,
il petto delle mamme tisiche
e l'odore –
odor di cenci, d'escrementi, di morti –
serpeggiante per tetri corridoi

sono una siepe che geme nel vento
fra me e te.   10

Ma fuori,
due grandi lumi fermi sotto stelle nebbiose
dicono larghi sbocchi
ed acqua
che va alla campagna;

e ogni lama di luce, ogni chiesa
nera sul cielo, ogni passo
di povere scarpe sfasciate

porta per strade d'aria
religiosamente   20
me a te.

27 febbraio 1938

Via dei Cinquecento*

There weigh between us two   I
too many words unspoken

and the hunger not relieved,
cries of babies not appeased,
the mothers' TB chests
and the smell –
smell of rags, of shit, of the dead –
snaking through dark corridors

are a hedge that groans in the wind
between me and you.   10

But outside,
two great lamps still under foggy stars
speak of wide clearings
and water
going into the country;

and each light blade, each black
church on the sky, each step
of poor broken shoes

bears through airy streets
religiously   20
me to you.

27th February 1938

Mattino

In riva al lago azzurro della vita   1
son corpi le nuvole bianche
dei figli carnosi del sole:

già l'ombra è alle spalle, catena
di monti sommersi.

E a noi petali freschi di rosa
infioran la mensa e son boschi
interi e verdi di castani smossi
nel vento delle chiome:

odi giunger gli uccelli?   10

Essi non hanno paura
dei nostri volti e delle nostre vesti
perché come polpa di frutto
siamo nati dall'umida terra.

Pasturo, 10 luglio 1938

Morning*

On the edge of life's blue lake   1
white clouds are bodies
of the sun's fleshy sons:

already the shadow's behind us, chain
of mountains submerged.

And to us fresh rose petals
adorn the table and they're whole
and green woods of chestnuts moved
in the wind at their fringes:

you hear the birds arriving?   10

They have no fear
of our faces and our clothes
because like fruit's pulp
we're born from the damp earth.

Pasturo, 10th July 1938

Per Emilio Comici

Si spalancano laghi di stupore   I
a sera nei tuoi occhi
fra lumi e suoni:

s'aprono lenti fiori di follia
sull'acqua dell'anima, a specchio
della gran cima coronata di nuvole...

Il tuo sangue che sogna le pietre
è nella stanza
un favoloso silenzio.

Misurina, 7 agosto 1938

For Emilio Comici*

Lakes of wonder are spread wide   I
at evening in your eyes
amidst lights and sounds:

slow flowers of folly open
on the spirit's waters, mirroring
the high peak crowned with clouds...

Your blood that dreams of the rocks
is a fairy-tale
silence in the room.

Misurina, 7th August 1938

LA VITA SOGNATA /
THE DREAMED LIFE*

La vita sognata

Chi mi parla non sa   1
che io ho vissuto un'altra vita –
come chi dica
una fiaba
o una parabola santa.

Perché tu eri
la purità mia,
tu cui un'onda bianca
di tristezza cadeva sul volto
se ti chiamavo con labbra impure,   10
tu cui lacrime dolci
correvano nel profondo degli occhi
se guardavamo in alto –
e così ti parevo più bella.

O velo
tu – della mia giovinezza,
mia veste chiara,
verità svanita –
o nodo
lucente – di tutta una vita   20
che fu sognata – forse –

oh, per averti sognata,
mia vita cara,
benedico i giorni che restano –
il ramo morto di tutti i giorni che restano,
che servono
per piangere te.

25 settembre 1933

The Dreamed Life

Who speaks to me won't know   1
I've lived another life –
as one who tells
a fairy tale
or a holy parable.

Because you were
my purity,
you with a white wave
of sadness fallen across your face
should I call you with impure lips,   10
you whose sweet tears
ran from the depths of eyes
if we were looking skyward –
and so I seemed the lovelier to you.

O you
veil – of my youth,
my light dress,
vanished truth –
O gleaming
knot – of a whole life   20
that was dreamed – perhaps –

oh, for having dreamed you,
my dear life,
I bless the days remaining –
the dead branch of all the days remaining,
that serve
to be mourning you.

25th September 1933

L'allodola

Dopo il bacio – dall'ombra degli olmi   1
sulla strada uscivamo
per ritornare:
sorridevamo al domani
come bimbi tranquilli.
Le nostre mani
congiunte
componevano una tenace
conchiglia
che custodiva   10
la pace.
Ed io ero piana
quasi tu fossi un santo
che placa la vana
tempesta
e cammina sul lago.
Io ero un immenso
cielo d'estate
all'alba
su sconfinate   20
distese di grano.
Ed il mio cuore
una trillante allodola
che misurava
la serenità.

25 agosto 1933

The Skylark

After the kiss – from the elms' shadow   1
on the road we'd come out
to return:
we were smiling at tomorrow
like tranquil children.
Our two hands
conjoined
composed a tenacious
seashell
that guarded over   10
peace.
And I was prostrate
as if you were a saint
who calms
the vain storm
and walks on the lake.
I was an immense
summer sky
at dawn
on the endless   20
extent of wheat.
And my heart
a trilling skylark
that measured
the serenity.

25th August 1933

La gioia

Domandavo a occhi chiusi   1
– che cosa
sarà domani la Pupa? –

Così ti facevo ridire
in un sorriso le dolci parole
– la sposa,
la mamma –

Fiaba
del tempo d'amore –
profondo sorso – vita   10
compiuta –
gioia ferma nel cuore
come un coltello nel pane.

26 settembre 1933

The Joy

With eyes closed I was asking you: 1
– so what will Baby
be tomorrow? –

So I made you say again
in a smile the sweet words:
– the bride,
a mother –

Fable
from the time of love –
profound sip – life   10
fulfilled –
joy firm in the heart
like a knife in bread.

26th September 1933

Ricongiungimento

Se io capissi   1
quel che vuole dire
– non vederti più –
credo che la mia vita
qui – finirebbe.

Ma per me la terra
è soltanto la zolla che calpesto
e l'altra
che calpesti tu:
il resto   10
è aria
in cui – zattere sciolte – navighiamo
a incontrarci.

Nel cielo limpido infatti
sorgono a volte piccole nubi
fili di lana
o piume – distanti –
e chi guarda di lì a pochi istanti
vede una nuvola sola
che si allontana.   20

17 settembre 1933

Rejoining

If I knew   1
what it would mean
– not to see you any more –
I believe my life
here – it would finish.

But for me the earth
is just the clod I trample
and the other
trampled by you:
the remainder   10
is air
in which – loosed raft – we sail
to meet together.

In fact in the limpid sky
at times there arise little wisps
threads of wool
or feathers – far off –
and who looks a moment later
sees a single cloud
going faraway.   20

17th September 1933

149

Inizio della morte

Quando ti diedi   1
le mie immagini di bimba
mi fosti grato: dicevi che era
come se io volessi
ricominciare la vita
per donartela intera.

Ora nessuno più
trae dall'ombra
la piccola lieve
persona che fu   10
in una breve
alba – la Pupa bambina:

ora nessuno si china
alla sponda
della mia culla obliata –

Anima –
e tu sei entrata
sulla strada del morire.

28 agosto 1933

Start of Death

When I gave to you   1
my baby pictures
you were grateful: said it was
as if I wanted
to begin life again
and give it you entire.

Now no one any longer
draws from shadow
the little slight
person who was   10
in a brief
dawn – the infant Babe:

now no one leans
over the side
of my forgotten crib –

Spirit –
and you'd entered
upon the road of dying.

28th August 1933

Saresti stato

Annunzio
saresti stato
di quel che non fummo,
di quello che fummo
e che non siamo più.

In te sarebbero
ritornati i morti
e vissuti i non nati,
sgorgate le acque
sepolte.

La poesia,
da noi amata e non sciolta
dal cuore mai,
tu l'avresti cantata
con gridi di fanciullo.

L'unica spiga
di due zolle confuse
eri tu –
lo stelo
della nostra innocenza
sotto il sole.

Ma sei rimasto laggiù,
con i morti,
con i non nati,
con le acque
sepolte –
alba già spenta al lume
delle ultime stelle:

You'd Have Been

Herald   1
you'd have been
of what we weren't,
of what we were
and are no more.

In you the dead
would have returned
and the unborn lived,
the entombed
waters gushed.   10

The poetry,
loved by us and never
loosed from the heart,
you'd have sung it
with boy's cries.

The single wheat ear
of two mixed clods
it was you –
the stem
of our innocence   20
under the sun.

But you've stayed down there
with the dead,
the unborn,
with entombed
waters –
dawn quenched already in the light
of the final stars:

non occupa ora terra
ma solo   30
cuore
la tua invisibile
bara.

22 ottobre 1933

now it doesn't take up earth
but only   30
heart
your invisible
bier.

22nd October 1933

Maternità

Pensavo di tenerlo in me, prima   1
che nascesse,
guardando il cielo, le erbe, i voli
delle cose leggere,
il sole –
perché tutto il sole
scendesse in lui.

Pensavo di tenerlo in me, cercando
d'essere buona –
buona –   10
perché ogni bontà
fatta sorriso
crescesse in lui.

Pensavo di tenerlo in me, parlando
spesso con Dio –
perché Dio lo guardasse
e noi fossimo
redenti in lui.

24 ottobre 1933

Maternity

I thought to hold him inside, before   1
he were born,
look to the sky, the grasses, the flights
of lightweight things,
the sun –
so that all the sun
would descend in him.

I thought to hold him inside, and try
to be good –
be good –   10
so that every goodness
become a smile
would grow in him.

I thought to hold him inside, and speak
often to God –
so that God would look over him
and us, we would be
redeemed in him.

24th October 1933

Il bimbo nel viale

Da quando io dissi – Il bimbo   1
avrà il nome del tuo fratello morto –

– era una sera d'ottobre, buia,
sotto grandi alberi, senza
vederci in viso –

egli fu vivo. E quando
nel viale sostavamo – ai nostri piedi
quieto giocava
con la ghiaia e gli insetti e le lievi
foglie cadute.   10

Per questo – lenti
erano i nostri passi e dolci –
così dolci – gli occhi
quando sul ciglio erboso
scorgevamo una margheritina
e sapevamo che un bimbo – sporgendo
appena il suo piccolo braccio –
può coglierla e non calpesta il prato.

25 ottobre 1933

The Boy on the Avenue

From when I said – the boy   1
will have your dead brother's name –

– it was an October evening, dark,
under great trees, unable to see
either of our faces –

he was alive. And when
on the avenue we stayed – at our feet
quiet he played
with gravel and insects and weightless
fallen leaves.   10

That's why – slow
and gentle our steps were –
so sweet – the eyes
when on a grassy slope
we found a tiny marguerite
and knew a child – just stretching
out his little arm –
could pick it and not tread down the meadow.

25th October 1933

Gli occhi del sogno

Tu mi dicevi: – Voglio   1
che il bambino abbia gli occhi come i tuoi –
Io mi toccavo le palpebre,
fissavo il cielo
per sentirmi lo sguardo
diventare più azzurro.
Tu mi dicevi: – Voglio
per questo
che tu non pianga –

Oh, per rispetto   10
di quello che fu tuo,
per amore
di quello che hai amato:
vedi, non piango –
vedi, i miei occhi – ancora
puri ed azzurri –
portano il raggio del sogno,
parlano ancora
di lui – con il cielo.

12 ottobre 1933

The Dream's Eyes

You'd tell me: – I want   1
the boy to have eyes like yours –
I'd touch my eyelashes,
would stare at the sky
to feel my gaze
become more blue.
You'd tell me: – I want
you not to cry
for this –

Oh, out of respect   10
for what was yours,
for the love
of what you'd loved:
see, I don't cry –
see, my eyes – still
pure and blue –
bear the dream's ray,
still speak
of him – with the sky.

12th October 1933

Voto

Ed è tanta la pace 1
ch'io dico:
– oh, possa tu incontrare la donna
che ti ridìa
la creatura che abbiamo sognata
e che è morta –
dico:
– si faccia solco
almeno per te
la fossa 10
e si confonda con la pioggia del cielo
il mio pianto:
bagni il tuo crescere
senza essere scorto –

8 settembre 1933

Vow

And the peace is such   1
that I say:
– oh, may you meet the woman
who would return to you
the creature we dreamed of
and who died –
I say:
– may the ditch become
at least for you
a furrow   10
and my own tears be blended
with rain from the sky:
may they water your growth
without being discerned –

8th September 1933

POESIE INEDITE /
UNCOLLECTED POEMS

Canto della mia nudità

Guardami: sono nuda. Dall'inquieto   1
languore della mia capigliatura
alla tensione snella del mio piede,
io sono tutta una magrezza acerba
inguainata in un color d'avorio.
Guarda: pallida è la carne mia.
Si direbbe che il sangue non vi scorra.
Rosso non ne traspare. Solo un languido
palpito azzurro sfuma in mezzo al petto.
Vedi come incavato ho il ventre. Incerta   10
è la curva dei fianchi, ma i ginocchi
e le caviglie e tutte le giunture,
ho scarne e salde come un puro sangue.
Oggi, m'inarco nuda, nel nitore
del bagno bianco e m'inarcherò nuda
domani sopra un letto, se qualcuno
mi prenderà. E un giorno nuda, sola,
stesa supina sotto troppa terra,
starò, quando la morte avrà chiamato.

Palermo, 20 luglio 1929

Song of My Nakedness*

Look at me: I'm naked. From   1
the unquiet languor of my hair
to the slim tension of my foot,
I'm all an unripe thinness
sheathed in an ivory colour.
Look: my flesh is pallid.
You'd say blood doesn't flow,
nor red shine through. Just a languid
blue beat blurs within my breast.
See how hollow my stomach is. Unsure   10
is the curve of my sides, but knees
and calves and all the joints
are lean and firm as a thoroughbred.
Today, I curve naked, in the clarity
of the white bath and I'll curve naked
on a bed tomorrow, if someone
will take me. And one day naked, alone,
stretched out under too much earth,
I'll be, when death has called me.

Palermo, 20th July 1929

L'ora di grazia

Tetraggine lenta, sfinita   1
di un cortile umidiccio
in maschera di giardino;
ostentata verdezza
di un fico sterile
che non sa né il vento né il sole;
malinconia di una piccola finestra a ogiva,
di un ballatoio ingombro di foglie morte,
di un povero tralcio nero inchiodato al muro
che sopra al ballatoio si sfa   10
in quattro pampini vizzi.
Qui l'ora di grazia non può essere
se non l'ora delle campane:
quando la sera, cantando,
si getta dalle torri incombenti
e come acqua ricolma
ogni fossa terrena;
quando su ogni stento terreno
che duole in maschera di ricchezza
la sera, come acqua, riflette,   20
dal cielo al fondo, qualche raggio di stella.

Milano, 7 novembre 1931

The Hour of Grace

Slow, exhausted gloom   1
of a dampish courtyard
in the guise of a garden;
shown off greenness
of a barren fig
that knows neither wind nor sun;
melancholy of a small ogive window,
of a gallery clogged with dead foliage,
of a poor black tendril nailed to the wall
that's done for above the gallery   10
in four withered vine leaves.
Here the hour of grace can't be
other than the hour of bells:
when the evening, singing,
is hurled from impending towers
and like water fills again
every earthly ditch;
when upon each wretched ground
that aches in the guise of wealth
the evening, like water, reflects,   20
from sky on down, some starry ray.

Milan, 7th November 1931

Inezie

Così – come di un povero bambino   1
che quando è morto bisogna
in mezzo al pianto pensare
a prender le misure della bara –
poi ci si mette d'accordo col fioraio
perché mandi il cuscino
e una bella corona –
– Rose bianche, narcisi, serenelle,
che cosa si usa mettere
sul carro di un bambino? –   10

Così – m'impegno oggi a cercare
come potrei inviarti
questi ultimi fiori dei miei prati –
se in un involto – oppure
in una piccola scatola –
in modo che non sembrino comprati
in un qualunque negozio –
in modo che tu possa riconoscere
le mie mani – su loro –
in modo che non debbano   20
– sopratutto – avvizzire –

Così vedi – frantumo
me stessa in tante povere
inezie
pietose
se m'impediscono di sentire
che questo è l'ultimo addio –
ch'io reco sulle mani il mio
amore morto –

Milano, 15 maggio 1933

Trifles*

Like so – as of a poor baby boy   1
how when it's dead you have
amid the tears to think
of measurements for the coffin –
then arrange with the florist
so that he send the pillow
and a beautiful crown –
– White roses, narcissi, lilac,
what do you use to put
on the bier of a child? –   10

Like so – I set myself to look
for how I could send you
these last flowers from my meadows –
if in a bundle – or else
in a little box –
in such a way they don't seem
bought in one shop or another –
in such a way you can recognize
my own hands – upon them –
in such a way they don't have   20
– above all – to wither –

Like so you see – I smash
myself up into many poor
pitiful
trifles
if they prevent me from sensing
that this is the final goodbye –
that I hold in my hands
my own dead love –

Milan, 15th May 1933

abbozzo

Io penso questa sera 1
alla leggenda dell'Uccello di Fuoco –
al suo apparire nel folto –
al suo canto liberatore –

e tutti narrano
del giovane principe
e del sonno dei nemici
e della sua salvezza –

nessuno pensa all'albero oscuro
dove l'uccello apparì 10
la prima sera –
nessuno pensa alla vita dell'albero
dopo quella sera
senza più la vampa
delle ali magiche –

io sola so
come l'albero viva
di nostalgia e d'attesa –
e intorno veda
la gente che si aggira – 20
ma nessuna veste variopinta
vale per lui
lo splendore
dell'Uccello scomparso –

l'albero non sa più
per chi sia il suo fiorire –
e per ogni foglia che nasce
si torce nelle intime fibre –
l'albero non sa più

draft*

This evening I think
of the Firebird legend –
its appearance in the thicket –
its liberator song –

and everyone tells
of the youthful prince
and the enemies' sleep
and of his escape –

no one thinks of the dark tree
where the bird appeared
the first evening –
no one thinks of the tree's life
after that evening
no longer with the blaze
of its magic wings –

only I know
how the tree lives
on nostalgia and waiting –
and around it sees
the people wander by –
but no multi-coloured clothes
equal for him
the splendour
of the vanished Bird –

the tree no longer knows
who its blossoming is for –
and for every leaf born
writhes in its intimate sinew –
the tree no longer knows

a chi offrire   30
il suo strazio primaverile –
e attende la notte –
la notte nera senza stelle senza fontane –
l'ora del buio silenzio –
quando dalle profonde radici
in un balenio estremo accecante
sorgerà correrà per il fusto
sino alla cima delle fronde –
unico bene suo –
il ricordo infuocato dell'Uccello –   40

marzo–agosto 1933

who to offer   30
its springtime torment –
and waits for night –
black night with no stars no fountains –
the hour of dark silence –
when from its deep roots
in a final blinding flash
there'll rise there'll run through its trunk
far as the tip of its fronds –
its only good –
the burning memory of the Bird –   40

March–August 1933

L'operaio delle luci

E sempre queste travi e questa polvere.   1
A volte
la tela ruvida dello scenario
si gonfia – accanto
alle mie mani, al mio viso.
Quando è stretta la scena
– una camera da letto –
la tela allora va distante:
c'e aria
qui intorno al mio quadrante   10
d'interruttori bianchi e neri.
Una sera
ho guardato dall'orlo del sipario:
c'erano siepi pallide di volti
come pani crudi
in attesa nel forno di velluto.
Stanotte dovrò spegnere le luci
a metà della scena d'amore:
arrossiranno
laggiù le facce smunte, continuando   20
sole in mezzo al frastuono
il desiderio
di quel che non s'avvera.

Mi passerà vicina, calda, bianca,
abbrividendo con le spalle nude
all'aria dei ventilatori:
credo
che sarà verde stasera la sua veste.

n.d.

The Lights Operator*

And these roof beams always and this dust.   1
At times
the rough cloth of the backdrop
swells out – beside
my hands, at my face.
When the scene is cramped
– a bedroom –
then the cloth goes far away:
there is air
here round my display   10
of black and white switches.
One evening
I looked from the fringe of the curtain:
there were pale rows of faces
like uncooked loaves
waiting in the velvet oven.
Tonight I'll have to cut the lights
halfway through the love scene:
emaciated features
will blush below, continuing   20
alone amid the uproar
the desire
for what doesn't come true.

She'll pass by me, heated, white,
shivering with naked shoulders
in the ventilators' air:
I believe
her costume will be green tonight.

Undated

Notes

My notes are thoroughly indebted to those in Antonia Pozzi, *Tutte le opere*, ed. Alessandra Cenni (Milan: Garzanti, 2009), where further information of an editorial kind can be found. I have also consulted the notes in Antonia Pozzi, *Breath: Poems and Letters*, trans. Lawrence Venuti (Middletown, CT: Wesleyan University Press, 2002), and those by Laura Barile in *Antologia della poesia italiana III: Ottocento-Novecento*, ed. Cesare Segre and Carlo Ossola (Turin: Einaudi, 1999), pp. 1280–88.

p. 5, *to A.M.C.*: Pozzi's Italian editors Alessandra Cenni and Onorina Dino restored this dedication to Antonio Maria Cervi, Pozzi's Classics teacher with whom she had an affair. The tomb is Annunzio Cervi's, brother of Antonio Maria, a poet and volunteer who died on 25th October 1918 on the Monte Grappa front a few days before the armistice. Annunzio Cervi's poetry, first collected in 1920, notably influenced Pozzi's earliest writing, above all for emotional reasons, but also because she was still in search of her own personal poetic timbre, as is natural in a teenager.

p. 7, *to L.B.*: Lucia Bozzi, great friend and confidante of the poet, a fellow pupil first at high school and then at university. Bozzi was the main recipient of manuscript drafts for many of Pozzi's poems, and, after the poet's death, she copied works from the notebooks, which were preserved and eventually donated to the archive, greatly contributing to the establishment of the complete oeuvre and the removal of editorial interventions by other hands.

p. 9, *Love of Distance*: Two initial lines were deleted by the poet: "*Sfumar le cose in una nebbia azzurra / anche se ostentano il più crudo verde*" ("Blurring things in an azure fog / even if they boast the crudest green").

p. 11, *to T.F.*: Perhaps Teresita Foschi, a high-school friend whose name and address appear among those of other students and professors on a notebook page.

p. 13, *the Montello*: A hillside on the river Piave front, where a number of bloody encounters took place in June 1918 during the German and Austro-Hungarian attack.

p. 15, *Santa Margherita*: A seaside town on the Ligurian coast not far from Portofino and Rapallo.

p. 17, *Carnisio*: A small village in Valcuvia, in Provincia di Varese.

p. 25, *The Closing Door*: The 1964 Mondadori edition of *Parole* removed the divisions between verses that had appeared in this poem in earlier texts. It also included the following edited version of the first eight lines: "*Tu lo vedi, sorella: io sono stanca – / come il pilastro d'un cancello angusto / diga nel tempo all'irruente fuga / d'una folla rinchiusa*" ("You see it, sister: I'm tired – / like the column of a strait gate / dyke through time to a headlong flight / of a hemmed-in crowd").

p. 29, *Kingston*: Kingston upon Thames is to the south-west of London, the place where Pozzi stayed during her English visit. Venuti notes that it was arranged to encourage the break-up of her relationship with Cervi.

p. 37, *Sunset*: Under the manuscript title another has been written, in pencil and in a different hand: 'Inverno' ('Winter'), which was adopted for the 1964 Mondadori edition.

p. 39, *the Cimon della Pala*: A pyramid-shaped stone outcrop in the western Dolomites near San Martino di Castrozza, where the poem appears to have been partially written.

p. 41, *White Light*: The poem remembers a cemetery in England over a year after Pozzi's sojourn there.

p. 51, *Path*: Over the autograph title, in Pozzi's father's handwriting, appears the title 'Lungo il torrente' ('Beside the Torrent'), which was adopted in the first Mondadori edition. The path and the gate are those of the cemetery in Pasturo.

p. 53, *Undated*: Though not dated, the poem was written between the compositions of 'Sentiero' on the 9th and 'Preghiera alla poesia' on the 23rd August 1934.

p. 57, *Scent of Green*: This poem was first collected in Pozzi and Sereni, *La giovinezza che non trova scampo* (1995). In both the poet's notebook and that of Lucia Bozzi it is cancelled in pencil.

p. 67, *Athens*: Both this and the following poem, 'Africa', derive from Pozzi's memories of a sea cruise in April 1934 in the company of her aunt Ida.

p. 71, *A Fate*: The poem was written on Antonia Pozzi's twenty-third birthday. The conclusion to her thesis on Flaubert's literary formation, completed in the same year, reads: "For those who, because of their position, can't struggle; for those who can't sacrifice themselves devoutly enough to a task; for those who cannot formulate, faced with their own destiny, a prayer of their own, these words, that bespeak a destiny and are a prayer, will be an eternal warning – we are alone. Alone like the Bedouin in the desert. We need to cover our face, to wrap ourselves tightly in our cloaks and to throw ourselves head down into the hurricane – and always, incessantly – until our last drop of water, until the last beat of our heart. When we die, we'll have this consolation: to have covered a certain ground and to have sailed in the Grand."

p. 79, *The Women*: Venuti notes the connection between this poem and the beginning of Mussolini's war in Eritrea in 1935.

p. 91, *Portofino*: A promontory fishing village, famous for its beauty, on the Ligurian coast near Rapallo, and which has now become a tourist resort.

p. 101, *Thirst*: Cenni notes in *Tutte le opere* (2009) that the text of this poem has been crossed out in pencil in Pozzi's notebook.

p. 111, *if the hill crest… sleeping upon them*: In the village of Pasturo the outline of the mountain facing the cemetery resembles, in the minds of the villagers, the profile of a sleeping child.

p. 125, *Still faces are intertwined… un-ruined smile of my years*: This second verse is ringed in pencil in Pozzi's notebook and is left out of the Mondadori edition.

p. 125, *Madonna di Campiglio*: A village in the Trentino Dolomites.

p. 135, *Via dei Cinquecento*: Venuti notes that this street in the outskirts of Milan is where the poet undertook voluntary social work during 1938, which included visiting tenements where the evicted found shelter.

p. 137, *Morning*: Entitled 'Pan' in the Mondadori edition, but Cenni gives authorial evidence for this title.

p. 139, *For Emilio Comici*: The poem is for the famous professional Alpine guide, who died in October 1940, during an exercise in the Val Gardena. Some manuscripts have the poem with an earlier title, 'Il rocciatore' ('The Rockclimber').

p. 141, *La vita sognata / The Dreamed Life*: The poems in this section, all from 1933, derive from the definitive end to the love affair between Pozzi and her teacher Antonio Maria Cervi, after the intervention of the poet's father in 1932. Much of Pozzi's work from 1933 relates to this episode. That she intended these poems to be seen together as a distinct group is clear from the fact that she wrote out their titles as a list in her notebook under the title *La vita sognata* on two occasions. Furthermore, loose-paper versions of nine of the ten poems (the exception being 'Il bimbo nel viale' – 'The Boy on the Avenue') were collected together by the poet with a cover on which is written "La vita sognata" and the date: 25th October 1933 – exactly fifteen years after the death of Annunzio Cervi, brother of Antonio Maria, in the closing days of the First World War. The lovers intended to name their first male child after this dead brother.

p. 167, *Song of My Nakedness*: This poem is cancelled in the poet's notebook, and the lack of manuscript copies and its absence from Lucia Bozzi's notebooks suggests repudiation by the author.

p. 171, *Trifles*: Cenni notes that in Pozzi's notebook the title and the text are crossed out.

p. 173, *draft*: According to Cenni the title of this poem appears in lower case in the notebook.

p. 177, *The Lights Operator*: This poem only exists in a pencil draft state among the loose manuscripts.

Select Bibliography

Works:
Antonia Pozzi, Flaubert: La formazione letteraria (1830–1856) (Milan: Garzanti, 1940)
—*Parole* (Milan: Mondadori, 1939), with enlarged editions in 1943, 1948 and 1964
—*La vita sognata e altre poesie inedite*, ed. Alessandra Cenni and Onorina Dino (Milan: Scheiwiller, 1986)
—*Diari*, ed. Alessandra Cenni and Onorina Dino (Milan: Scheiwiller, 1988)
—*Parole*, ed. Alessandra Cenni and Onorina Dino (Milan: Garzanti, 1989), with further editions in 1998, 2001 and 2004
—*L'età delle parole è finita: Lettere 1927–1938*, ed. Alessandra Cenni and Onorina Dino (Milan: Rosellina Archinto, 1989)
—and Vittorio Sereni, *La giovinezza che non trova scampo: Poesie e lettere degli anni trenta*, ed. Alessandra Cenni (Milan: Scheiwiller, 1995)
—*Mentre tu dormi le stagioni passano…*, ed. Alessandra Cenni and Onorina Dino (Milan: Viennepierre edizioni, 1998)
—*Poesia, mi confesso con te: Ultime poesie inedite (1929–1933)*, ed. Onorina Dino (Milan: Viennepierre edizioni, 2004)
—*Tutte le opere*, ed. Alessandra Cenni (Milan: Garzanti, 2009)
—*Poesia che mi guardi*, ed. Graziella Bernabò and Onorina Dino (Bologna: Sossella, 2010), published with a 2009 film by Marina Spada

English Translations:
Antonia Pozzi, *Poems*, trans. Nora Wydenbruck (London: John Calder, 1955)
—*Breath: Poems and Letters*, trans. Lawrence Venuti (Middletown, CT: Wesleyan University Press, 2002)

Biographies:
Alessandra Cenni, *In riva alla vita: Storia di Antonia Pozzi poetessa* (Milan: Rizzoli, 2002)
Graziella Bernabò, *Per troppa vita che ho nel sangue: Antonia Pozzi e la sua poesia* (Milan: Viennepierre edizioni, 2004)

Criticism:
For a listing of Italian criticism, see *Tutte le opere*, pp. 663–70.

Index of Titles

ITALIAN TITLES

INDEX OF TITLES

Peter Robinson is Professor of English and American Literature at the University of Reading. Among his many volumes of poetry, translations and literary criticism are *Selected Poems* (2003), *The Look of Goodbye: Poems 2001-2006* (2008), *English Nettles and Other Poems* (2010), *Selected Poetry and Prose of Vittorio Sereni* (2006), *The Greener Meadow: Selected Poems of Luciano Erba* (2007), awarded the John Florio Prize, and *Poetry & Translation: The Art of the Impossible* (2010). He has also recently edited Bernard Spencer's *Complete Poetry, Translations & Selected Prose* (2011) and *Reading Poetry: An Anthology* (2011).

ALMA CLASSICS

ALMA CLASSICS aims to publish mainstream and lesser-known European classics in an innovative and striking way, while employing the highest editorial and production standards. By way of a unique approach the range offers much more, both visually and textually, than readers have come to expect from contemporary classics publishing.

To order any of our titles and for up-to-date information about our current and forthcoming publications, please visit our website on:

www.almaclassics.com